SOCIOLOGY

AND THE

MILITARY ESTABLISHMENT

Prepared for the
American Sociological Society

By MORRIS JANOWITZ
Department of Sociology
The University of Michigan

RUSSELL SAGE FOUNDATION

New York   1959

© 1959

RUSSELL SAGE FOUNDATION

Printed in the United States
of America

Printed April, 1959
Reprinted August, 1960
Reprinted August, 1962

*Library of Congress
Catalog Card Number: 59–10151*

WM. F. FELL CO., PRINTERS
PHILADELPHIA, PA.

Michael G. Hanemann

CONTENTS

FOREWORD

WORLD WAR II marked the first time that sociologists were employed in their professional capacity by the military establishment of this country. Except for the few serving in intelligence research and in political warfare propaganda operations, sociologists engaged in military research during that period were largely concerned with attitude and opinion studies relevant to the general problems of morale and personnel management.

Postwar military interest in the possible contributions of sociologists has been characterized by acute, and sometimes critical, fluctuations. However, some of the wartime type of sociological research has continued. In addition, there have been occasional research studies on other problems, such as those pertaining to cold war political warfare, the social aspects of small unit efficiency, leadership and control patterns, and the social structure and cultural aspects of military organizations. Even so, there still seems to be no clear conception on the part of the Department of Defense, or for that matter, most sociologists, of the possibilities of military sociology as an important contributor to military effectiveness. There is, for example, as yet only minimal evidence of awareness of the need for persistent and systematic research on the nature of military organizational systems and on the processes and problems involved in the fundamental changes that our own system is undergoing.

The American Sociological Society and Russell Sage Foundation, joint sponsors of this bulletin on military sociology, believe that it will serve to impress upon sociologists and professional military officials alike the need for more effective utilization of sociological theory and research capability in the analysis of problems of vital importance to our military forces.

While this bulletin emphasizes the importance to the military organization of more effective utilization of sociological theory and research, it also makes evident that research on military problems would provide extremely valuable opportunities for testing sociological theory and method.

Neither the sponsors nor the author conceive this report to be an intensive review and appraisal of all research in the field of military sociology. Rather, the intention is to stimulate the development of more adequate conceptions of the basic sociological problems presented by the United States military institution, its internal functioning, and its relation to the total social system. Given the broadened perspective indicated in these pages, it is our belief that the trend toward an intelligent and comprehensive application of sociology to military problems will be greatly accelerated.

In the preparation of this bulletin, Dr. Janowitz had the benefit of advice from a committee appointed by the American Sociological Society and from members of the Foundation staff. The advisory committee consisted of Raymond W. Bowers, chairman of the Department of Sociology, University of Georgia; John W. Riley, Jr., chairman of the Department of Sociology, Rutgers University; M. Brewster Smith, Department of Psychology, New York University; Hans Speier, The Rand Corporation; Samuel A. Stouffer, Department of Social Relations, Harvard University; Robin M. Williams, Jr., chairman of the Department of Sociology and Anthropology, Cornell University.

This bulletin is the fourth of a series of bulletins, each dealing with a single area in which the sociologist is a practitioner or his work is relevant to practice. Bulletins already published in this series are: *Sociology and the Field of Corrections* by Lloyd E. Ohlin; *Sociology and the Field of Mental Health* by John A. Clausen; and *Sociology and the Field of Education* by Orville G. Brim, Jr. In preparation are the following: *Sociology and the Field of Social Work* by Henry J. Meyer and *Sociology and Medical Practice* by Albert F. Wessen.

LEONARD S. COTTRELL, JR.

Russell Sage Foundation
January 1, 1959

INTRODUCTION

IN SEEKING TO APPRAISE the present state and the outlook for sociological analysis of the military establishment, I have addressed myself to three tasks.

First, it was necessary to evaluate the published and unpublished research literature. The available published literature is not sufficient to permit an extensive codification that would give an adequate portrayal of military institutions in the United States. The results of government-sponsored research into "human resources" have produced a variety of unpublished documents most of which were surveyed. While these documents supplied relevant background materials, only a minor fraction was relevant or suitable for inclusion.

Instead, the second objective became paramount, namely, outlining and analyzing the main organizational trends at work in transforming the military establishment. Much of this bulletin therefore consists of suggested hypotheses and lines of inquiry based on my personal experiences. The all too few interested social scientists—in government and in university life—have freely discussed with me their observations about the transformation of military life. Of particular relevance were the observations of a handful of professional officers who have had the opportunity to study social science at civilian graduate schools.

In some respects, this bulletin can be considered to be a by-product of my forthcoming study on *The Professional Soldier*, which has been undertaken with the assistance of a grant-in-aid from the Social Science Research Council. In the course of that research which seeks to investigate the impact of the changing military profession on American political behavior in international relations, it became clear that a more comprehensive

7

picture of the internal social organization of the military establishment was first required. A variety of problem areas outlined
in this bulletin will be more fully dealt with in the larger study.

Finally, the third task was an interpretive statement of the
problems of applying the sociological perspective to the military
establishment. As yet, sociological analysis of the military establishment is not a standard part of the academic curriculum, nor
is it a subject for empirical research like other institutions in our
society. In discussing these problematic issues, I have been forced
necessarily well beyond the available documentation.

My major focus has been on the internal social organization of
the military establishment; hierarchy and authority, assimilation
of military roles, primary groups, and techniques of organizational control. But any analysis of the internal structure of an
institution requires attention to the social context. At best, I
could do no more than make essential assumptions about the
trends in modern society—technological, social, and ideological
—which influence military organization. I have excluded analysis
of interservice rivalries. These rivalries are not mainly an internal
military problem. Understanding of interservice rivalry involves
seeing it in terms of civilian political arrangements for determining military policy and the role of industrial organizations as
pressure groups on the military establishment. The mechanisms
of interservice rivalries also receive considerable attention in the
literature of political scientists. Likewise, the immense topic of the
social effects of war is not a central focus.

All organizations undergo continuous change, or at least this
is the assumption of the sociological perspective. It is a commonplace that in the contemporary decade the military establishment
is undergoing a radical transformation. The transformation is
grounded in the fantastic revolution in weapons, and is accom-
panied by the occurrence of a permanently expanded military
profession. Yet the sociological analysis of the military establishment is not a record of contemporary history. It is at the same
time something more and something less than such a record. It is
something less in the sense that it is not an effort to record in
detail the organizational structure and the elaborate administra-

tive arrangements which the military has developed. It is something more in the sense that it seeks to identify those organizational factors which are believed to be crucial in assisting and preventing adaptive change.

There exists considerable confusion about the sociological study of administrative behavior. The sociological analysis is sometimes thought to be too general and too abstract to be of relevance for guiding constructive problem-solving. Contrariwise, the argument is raised that administrative processes defy explication into generalized propositions. Both views are overdrawn stereotypes, in my opinion. Only the naive would believe that generalized knowledge will replace connoisseurship in the management of complex organizations. Contrariwise, expert administrative leaders are experts only to the degree that they are concerned continually with new sources of systematic information about their establishments. It is the task of the sociologist to demonstrate that research knowledge adds an increment to understanding beyond common sense observation. It was with such an objective that this bulletin was prepared.

MORRIS JANOWITZ

Center for Advanced Study
in the Behavioral Sciences
Stanford, California
December, 1958

I

THE MILITARY ESTABLISHMENT
AS A SOCIAL SYSTEM

It is appropriate to inquire why sociological literature on military organization is so undeveloped as compared, for example, with that on industrial and factory organization. Considerable effort has been expended by social scientists—almost exclusively personnel and social psychologists—on very selected and specific aspects of military life. During World War I a relatively new approach to the use of military personnel was stimulated by social research, namely, the importance of considering a person's intelligence, skills, and aptitudes in assigning him to a military occupation. The experiences of military psychologists of this period provided a basis for the subsequent rapid development of personnel selection in civilian industry and business.

For better or for worse, during World War II, an elaborate machinery was erected for matching men's skills to the jobs required. No large-scale organization as vast as the military establishment can operate without a standardized personnel selection system. But any personnel testing procedure runs the risk of developing overspecialization in both training procedures and personnel. It has even been argued that military personnel selection, as administered during World War II, resulted in draining off superior talent from essential but "unglamorous" assignments, such as the infantry. Moreover, no responsible personnel selector will claim that the dimensions of aggressive leadership in combat or strategic command have been satisfactorily conceptualized to the point where reliable personnel testing is possible.

Thus, it was understandable that during World War II social scientists broadened their interests beyond personnel selection and stressed the importance of research into motives and attitudes as aspects of military life. Research on "morale" was by no means a new approach to the management of complex and large-scale organizations. But the armed forces, that is, the ground and air forces, undertook morale studies on a most extensive scale. In the summary study of these efforts, *The American Soldier*,[1] prepared under the guidance of Samuel A. Stouffer, the potentialities and limitations of attitude and morale research are assessed. While a systematic evaluation of the consequences of these data on actual past operations or their relevance for military organization in the future was outside the scope of these volumes, illustrative implications, especially dealing with demobilization procedures, are presented. And again, as with the development of personnel selection during World War I, industry and business have continued the morale study as a tool of administrative management.

"Morale" versus Organization

Social research on attitudes and morale in the armed forces provides useful information for specific problems where it is assumed that the execution of a policy requires cooperation. The limitation of attitude research is not that the strategy and tactics of war cannot be based on the preferences of soldiers. This is obvious to all, including the social scientist. But, in fact, attitude research fails to describe the underlying social system—the realities of bureaucratic organization—of the armed forces. "Morale" is much too limited a concept to understand the coercive forces of bureaucratic organization, especially of military formations as they operate in combat. The findings of *The American Soldier* studies serve to underline and reaffirm this sociological observation:

> Thus we are forced to the conclusion that personal motives and relationships are not uniquely determinate for organization in combat . . . officers and men must be motivated to make the organization work, but not *all* of them have to be so motivated, nor must they all agree on details of social philosophy or be bound by ties of per-

Notes appear at the end of the respective chapters.

sonal friendship in order for a functioning organization to exist. To put it another way, the best single predictor of combat behavior is the simple fact of institutionalized role: knowing that a man is a soldier rather than a civilian. The soldier role is a vehicle for getting a man into the position in which he has to fight or take the institutionally sanctioned consequences.[2]

A potential model for analyzing the military establishment as a social system is represented by social research into industrial organization, which has a broader tradition than personnel selection and morale studies. Intellectual influences from historical writings, economic analysis, social anthropology, and sociological theory have emphasized the need for a comprehensive focus on the totality of industrial organization, not merely on part of it. The single concept of "morale" is displaced by a theory of organizational behavior in which an array of sociological concepts are employed: authority, communications, hierarchy, sanction, status, social role, allocation, and integration. Industrial organizations have common patterns of behavior which can be traced to similarities in their technological apparatus and to their goals of profits and productivity. Alternatively, variations in industrial behavior can be linked to the cultural, ideological, and political facets of any particular society. The sociological perspective toward the industrial establishment has produced a wide variety of rich theoretical treatises and empirical case studies on the internal administration of the factory system, and on the impact of industrial organization on contemporary social structure.[3]

By contrast, there exists no adequate sociological statement on contemporary American military organization, although fragmentary theoretical essays and particularistic research studies abound.[4] One might assume that sociologists' aspirations for an understanding of modern social structures would force them into a concern with military institutions which so thoroughly pervade contemporary society. The absence of a sustained interest in military institutions is manifested in all phases of sociological effort, including the standard introductory sociological text. Only in the writings of such leading political sociologists as Harold D.

Lasswell and Hans Speier has there been a continuing and systematic concern with the implications of military organization as agents of social change.[5] One of the most insightful and penetrating analyses of American military behavior is contained in *Men Against Fire* by Brigadier General S. L. A. Marshall (Ret.).[6] Since he is a professional newspaper writer and a military historian, his writings are not explicitly sociological, but they are based on an intimate understanding of military social organization. Through data from group interviews with World War II soldiers immediately after combat and on direct observation of battle performance, Marshall sought to account for the low expenditure of firepower by combat units (less than one-quarter of the troops fired their weapons in battle).

Interestingly enough, the operational requirements of political warfare against the German and Japanese armed forces led to research efforts in which these forces were regarded as total social systems. During World War II two social science units, working independently, recast operational and strategic intelligence into sociological models for explaining the strength and vulnerability of the Axis armed forces as they came under allied attack.[7] Their findings, as well as those reported in *The American Soldier*, showed high convergence in underscoring the central importance of primary group solidarity even in totalitarian armies as a crucial source of military effectiveness. Specifically, a social system perspective helped to focus attention on the important conclusion that it was not Nazi ideology which was at the root of German fanatical resistance, but rather the military and organizational practices which the Nazis permitted, encouraged, and required.

In explaining the absence of a realistic interest in military institutions, professional sociologists are prone to argue that the military has resisted organizational studies, and particularly organizational studies that have sought to reach into the upper levels of military management. This is a partially correct observation, which is basically irrelevant. The assent of the military would facilitate sociological inquiry, but such assent is hardly indispensable. Some of the best analyses of industrial sociology have come from documentary and secondary sources, participant observation, and the careful use of informants—reluctant or otherwise.

In part, this defense by sociologists is incorrect. The military establishment, as will be pointed out in this bulletin, has invited and subsidized social scientists to investigate the fundamental problems of military organization. It is true that all too often this support has been sporadic and based on an exaggerated notion of the potentialities of social science. Some of these efforts have produced relevant results. However, many major endeavors have resulted in unfinished research, unpublished mimeographed reports of pilot projects, or trivial research contributions, which indicate that failures in contract research have in part been due to the social scientist.

The explanation for the present absence of sociological analysis of the military establishment is more fundamental. In the United States the development of the social sciences is linked to the liberal tradition which, in general, has sought to handle the problem of military institutions by denial. There has been an understandable but fundamental tension between the professional soldier and the scholar, who seeks to apply the scientific method to the human side of military organization and armed conflict. The professional soldier often sees the social scientist as naive, even though he must defer to him because of professional courtesy. The social scientist sees the professional soldier as dogmatic. As a result, the approach of the social scientist to the military establishment has been segmental and technical, rather than comprehensive and scientific.

Bureaucracy: Civilian or Military

As a social organization, the contemporary military establishment has for some time tended to display more and more of the characteristics typical of any large-scale nonmilitary bureaucracy. The decreasing difference is a result of continuous technological change which vastly expands the size of the military establishment, increases its interdependence with civilian society, and alters its internal social structure. These technological developments in war-making require more and more professionalization. At the same time, the impact of military technology during the past half-century can be described in a series of propositions about social change. Each of the conditions symbolized by these propositions has had the effect of "civilizing" military institutions and of blurring the distinction between the civilian and the military.

1. An increasing percentage of the national income of a modern nation is spent for the preparation, execution, and repair of the consequences of war. Thus, there is a trend toward total popular involvement in the consequences of war and war policy, since the military establishment is responsible for the distribution of a progressively larger share of the available economic values.

2. Military technology both vastly increases the destructiveness of warfare and widens the scope of automation in new weapons. It is a commonplace that both of these trends tend to weaken the distinction between military roles and civilian roles as the destructiveness of war has increased. Weapons of mass destruction socialize danger to the point of equalizing the risks of warfare for both soldier and civilian. As long as the armed forces must rely on large numbers of drafted personnel, powerful influences toward civilianization are at work.

3. The revolution in military technology means that the military mission of deterring violence becomes more and more central as compared with preparing to apply violence. This shift in mission tends to civilianize military thought and organization as military leaders concern themselves with broad ranges of political, social, and economic policies.

4. The previous periodic character of the military establishment (rapid expansion, rapid dismantlement) has given way to a more permanent maintenance or expansion. The permanent character of the military establishment has removed one important source of civilian-military conflict, namely, the civilian tendency to abandon the military establishment after a war. Instead, because of the high rate of technological change, internal conflicts between the military services have been multiplied.

5. The complexity of the machinery of warfare and the requirements for research, development, and technical mainte-

nance tend to weaken the organizational boundary between the military and the nonmilitary, since the maintenance and manning of new weapons require a greater reliance on civilian-oriented technicians.

6. Given the "permanent" threat of war, it is well recognized that the tasks which military leaders perform tend to widen. Their technological knowledge, their direct and indirect power, and their heightened prestige result in their entrance, of necessity, into arenas that in the recent past have been reserved for civilian and professional politicians. The need that political and civilian leaders have for expert advice from professional soldiers about the strategic implications of technological change serves to mix the roles of the military and the civilian.

Nevertheless, the typical sociological analysis of military organization does not take into account the consequences of these trends and instead continues to emphasize authoritarian, stratified-hierarchical, and traditional dimensions as a basis for distinguishing the military from the nonmilitary bureaucracy.[8]

Thus, for example, Campbell and McCormack in their study "Military Experience and Attitudes Toward Authority,"[9] set out with the assistance of a United States Air Force research contract to prove that air cadet training would increase authoritarian predispositions among the officer candidates. Since they assumed that the dominant characteristics of a military organization are its authoritarian procedures, the consequences of participation in its training program necessarily heighten authoritarian personality tendencies among those who successfully pass through such training. Appropriately, authoritarian personality tendencies imply both the predisposition to dominate arbitrarily others of lower status and simultaneously to submit to arbitrary higher authority. When the results of the research, as measured by the well-known authoritarian "F" scale, showed a decrease in authoritarian traits among cadets after one year of training, the authors were tempted to conclude that perhaps their research tools were inadequate.[10] Direct examination of the organizational processes of combat flight training would indicate an emphasis on group interdependence and on a team concept of coordination to ensure survival that should have cautioned these researchers not to make the predictions they did make.[11]

The view with which these social scientists approached the military establishment is partly an expression of civilian ideology. Moreover, as Hans Speier points out in his critique of the *The American Soldier* research series, such a view distorts actual differences between military and civilian organization, since it overlooks what is common to large-scale organization in general.[12] Many of the "bureaucratic" features of military life are, in fact, to be found in civilian organizations in varying degree.

Combat Goals

These observations do not deny the crucial differences that exist between military and nonmilitary bureaucracies. The goals of an organization supply a meaningful basis for understanding differences in organizational behavior. The military establishment as a social system has unique characteristics because the possibility of hostilities is a permanent reality to its leadership. The fact that thermonuclear weapons alter the role of force in international relations does not deny this proposition. The consequences of preparation for future combat and the results of previous combat pervade the entire organization. The unique character of the military establishment derives from the requirement that its members are specialists in making use of violence and mass destruction. In the language of the soldier, this is recognized on a common sense basis: military mission is the key to military organization.

Changing technology creates new patterns of combat, and thereby modifies organizational behavior and authority in the military establishment. The narrowing distinction between military and nonmilitary bureaucracies can never result in the elimination of fundamental organizational differences. Three pervasive requirements for combat set limits to these civilianizing tendencies.

First, while it is true that modern warfare exposes the civilian and the soldier to more equal risks, the distinction between military roles and civilian roles has not been eliminated. Traditional combat-ready military formations need to be maintained for limited warfare. The necessity for naval and air units to carry on the hazardous tasks of continuous and long-range reconnaissance and detection, demand organizational forms that will bear the stamp of conventional formations. In the future, even with fully automated missile systems, conventional units must be maintained as auxiliary forces for the delivery of new types of weapons.

More important, no military system can rely on expectation of victory based on the initial exchange of firepower—whatever the form of the initial exchange may be. Subsequent exchanges will involve military personnel—again regardless of their armament—who are prepared to carry on the struggle as soldiers, that is, subject themselves to military authority and to continue to fight. The automation of war civilianizes wide sectors of the military establishment; yet the need to maintain combat readiness and to develop centers of resistance after initial hostilities ensures the continued importance of military organization and authority.

Second, what about the consequences of the increased importance of deterrence as a military mission? Should one not expect that such a shift also would result in civilianizing the military establishment? If the military is forced to think about deterring wars rather than fighting wars, the traditions of the "military mind," based on the inevitability of hostilities, must change and military authority must undergo transformation as well. There can be no doubt that this shift in mission is having important effects on military thought and organization. In fact, military pacifism is a growing and important trend in modern society as the horrors of war force military leaders to concern themselves with the political consequences of violence.

Again, there are limits to the consequences of this civilianizing trend. The role of deterrence is not a uniquely new mission for the military establishment. Historically, the contribution of the military to the balance of power has not been made because of the civilian character of the military establishment. To the contrary, the balance of power formula operates, when it does, because the military establishment is prepared to fight effectively and immediately.

With the increase in the importance of deterrence, military elites become more and more involved in diplomatic and political warfare, regardless of their preparation for such tasks. Yet the specific and unique contribution of the military to deterrence is the threat of violence which has currency; that is, it can be taken seriously because of the real possibility of violence. Old or new types of weapons do not alter this basic formula. In short, deterrence still requires organization prepared for combat.

Third, the assumption that military institutions, as compared with economic and industrial institutions, are resistant to technological change is considerably undermined as the process of innovation in the military establishment itself has become routinized. Nevertheless, as long as imponderables weigh heavy in estimating military outcomes and as long as the "fighter" spirit is required to face combat, the military rejects the civilian engineer as its professional model. Of course, the engineer is held in high esteem, but the ideal image of the military continues to be the strategic commander, not the military technician. It is the image of a leader, motivated by national patriotism and not by personal monetary gain, who is capable of organizing the talents of specialists for all types of contingencies.

The question of relative resistance to technological innovation by the military, as compared with civilian economic and industrial organization, has produced volumes of historical writing. In his broad historical survey John U. Nef argues that military organization and the requirements of war-making were not crucial factors in Western technological development and, therefore, were not mechanisms for stimulating economic development.[13]

In all probability, military organization as late as the middle of the nineteenth century was strongly resistant to technological innovation. Until that time the military establishments of Western Europe were dominated by aristocratic elements that were concerned with a traditional way of life. These elements stood in opposition to social change and technological innovation, and accepted new developments in military organization with great reluctance.

However, in the middle of the twentieth century, military institutions can no longer be thought of as merely reacting to external pressures and resisting technological innovation. For the sociologists studying the military establishment, it is important to emphasize that the armed forces now create their own requirements for technological innovation, which in turn influence industrial organization. The classical view of the military standing in opposition to technological innovation is inapplicable as the present cycle of the arms race converts the armed forces into centers of support for the development of new weapons systems. The military establishment hardly presents the ideal conditions for the professional scientist or the research engineer. Yet military leaders, regardless of the validity of their professional judgments about technological matters, are not characterized by traditional thinking about technological requirements.

Likewise, the procedures of innovation in industry and in the military tend to converge; increasing specialization involves the replacement of individual entrepreneurship by staff work and group research. In the contemporary military establishment with its continuous rotation of persons through official roles, the process of assessment of needs and prospects of technological innovation is as routinized and automatic as in civilian industry.

Leadership based on traditional military customs must share power with experts not only in technical matters but also in matters of organization and human relations. Specific organizational adaptations of the military even foreshadow developments in civilian society, since the military must press hard for innovation and respond more rapidly to social change. For example, the continued need for retraining personnel from operational to managerial positions and from older to newer techniques has led to a more rational spreading of higher education throughout the career of the military officer, rather than the concentrated dosage typical of the civilian in graduate or professional school.

No bureaucracy ever conforms to the ideal model of the rational organization and certainly the military establishment cannot be thought of in purely engineering terms. As long as "the battle is the pay off"—as long as there are dangerous and irksome tasks to be performed—an engineering philosophy cannot suffice as the organizational basis of the armed forces. Especially in a free enterprise, profit-motivated society, the military establishment is oriented to duty and honor. S. L. A. Marshall's observations touch directly on this essential theme of military life:

> A note of smugness was not missing from the remark all too frequently heard during World War II: "We go at this thing just like it was a great engineering job." What was usually overlooked was that to the men who were present at the pay off, it wasn't an engineering job, and had they gone about their duty in that spirit, there would have been no victory for our side.[14]

In a period of fantastic technological change, military leadership is confronted with an almost perpetual crisis of organization. The sociological analyst is concerned with understanding the organizational consequences of these technological changes. Yet it can be assumed that neither the increased automation of military technology, nor the military shift in mission from warmaking to deterrence, nor the decline in the traditional military opposition to innovation can produce a complete civilianization of the military establishment. The structure of military authority —the key to military organization—is an expression of the unique goals of the military, namely, combat and combat preparation.

In terms of manpower and mass destruction, air power is the ascendant arm, while ground and sea power remain the essential components of a system of graduated deterrence. The diversification and specialization of military technology lengthens the formal training required to gain mastery of military technology. The temporary citizen soldier, sailor, and aviator will become less important and a completely professional armed force more vital. The need to fight limited wars or strategic wars instantly, with the available mobilized forces, tends to increase reliance on a professional military establishment. But these contemporary trends do not produce a professional army isolated and remote from civilian society, but a military establishment that is an integral part of the larger society on which its technological resources depend.

NOTES TO CHAPTER I

[1] Stouffer, Samuel A., and others, *The American Soldier*. Princeton University Press, Princeton, N. J., 1949, vols. 1 and 2.

[2] *Ibid.*, vol. 2, p. 101.

[3] The main impetus for these analyses of the industrial establishment has not been the immediate solution of any practical problem. Rather, it is that an understanding of contemporary society is impossible without such an interest.

[4] Efforts in this direction are contained in Andrzejewski, Stanislaw, *Military Organization and Society*, Routledge and Kegan Paul, London, 1954; Williams, Richard Hays, *Human Factors in Military Operations:* Some Applications of the Social Sciences to Operations Research, Technical Memorandum ORO-T-259, Operations Research Office, Chevy Chase, Md., 1954, mimeographed; *Report of the Working Group on Human Behavior Under Conditions of Military Service:* A Joint Project of the Research and Development Board and the Personnel Policy Board in the Office of the Secretary of Defense, Washington, June, 1951; van Doorn, Jac A. A., *Sociologie van de Organisatie:* Beshouwingen over Organiseren in het Bizonder Gebaseerd op een Onderzoeck van het Militaire System, H. E. Stenfert Kroese, Leiden, 1956.

[5] Lasswell, Harold, *Politics:* Who Gets What, When, How, The Free Press, Glencoe, Ill., 1951; Speier, Hans, *Social Order and the Risks of War*, George W. Stewart, New York, 1952.

[6] Marshall, S. L. A., *Men Against Fire*. William Morrow and Co., New York, 1947.

[7] Leighton, Alexander, *Human Relations in a Changing World*, E. P. Dutton and Co., New York, 1949; Shils, Edward A., and Morris Janowitz, "Cohesion and Disintegration in the Wehrmacht in World War II," *Public Opinion Quarterly*, vol. 12, Summer, 1948, pp. 280–315.

[8] Stouffer, Samuel A., and others, *op. cit.*, vol. 1, p. 55; Davis, Arthur K., "Bureaucratic Patterns in the Navy Officer Corps," *Social Forces*, vol. 27, December, 1948, pp. 143–153; Rose, Arnold M., "The Social Structure of the Army," *American Journal of Sociology*, vol. 51, March, 1946, pp. 361–364; Freeman, Felton D., "The Army as a Social Structure," *Social Forces*, vol. 27, October, 1948, pp. 78–83; Brotz, Howard, and Everett Wilson, "Characteristics of Military Society," *American Journal of Sociology*, vol. 51, March, 1946, pp. 371–375; Spindler, G. Dearborn, "The Military—A Systematic Analysis," *Social Forces*, vol. 27, October, 1948, pp. 83–88; Page, Charles H., "Bureaucracy's Other Face," *Social Forces*, vol. 25, October, 1946, pp. 88–94.

[9] Campbell, Donald T., and Thelma H. McCormack, "Military Experiences and Attitudes Toward Authority," *American Journal of Sociology*, vol. 62, March, 1957, pp. 482–490. The data were collected for this study during the period January, 1953, to March, 1954.

[10] Adorno, T. W., and others, *The Authoritarian Personality*. Harper and Bros., New York, 1950, pp. 222–280.

[11] In fact, there is some empirical evidence, as well as ample observations, that selection boards in the Air Force tend to select for promotion the less authoritarian officers, presumably in part through selecting well-liked men. See E. P. Hollander's "Authoritarianism and Leadership Choice in a Military Setting," *Journal of Abnormal and Social Psychology*, vol. 49, July, 1954, pp. 365–

370. Richard Christie found only a slight and statistically insignificant increase in authoritarianism (California F scale) among a group of Army inductees after six weeks of infantry basic training; see *American Psychologist*, "Changes in Authoritarianism as Related to Situational Factors," vol. 7, June, 1952, pp. 307–308.

[12] Speier, Hans, "The American Soldier and the Sociology of Military Organization" in *Studies in the Scope and Method of "The American Soldier,"* edited by Robert K. Merton and Paul F. Lazarsfeld. The Free Press, Glencoe, Ill., 1950, pp. 106–132.

[13] Nef, John U., *War and Human Progress*. Harvard University Press, Cambridge, Mass., 1950.

[14] Marshall, S. L. A., *op. cit.*, p. 210.

II

HIERARCHY AND AUTHORITY

Hɪᴇʀᴀʀᴄʜʏ is the hallmark of a sociological conception of bureaucratic organization. The principle of hierarchy is simply that
every lower office is under the control and supervision of a higher
one. Since by definition the military establishment is a comprehensive and an all-embracing hierarchy, the career soldier is
assumed to be an ideal example of the professional operating
under bureaucratic authority. The contemporary growth of
bureaucratic organization in government, industry, and education implies the growth of this same hierarchical principle, historically associated with military life.

For the professional officer who has a career commitment to
the military, or for the selective service recruit scheduled to spend
a two-year tour of duty, military hierarchy operates pervasively.
The professional officer has entered on a career that attaches him
to a single authority through which all of his life chances are
regulated. The recruit finds that the full cycle of his daily
existence is now for the first time under the control of a single
authority. Military life is, in short, institutional life.

But it is the sources from which military authority derives
power and influence that are of crucial consequence. Does
authority flow from custom, law, or the personal characteristics of
key officer, to mention the categories of analysis offered by Max
Weber? Of course, no hierarchical organization of any size or
complexity has its authority system based on a single principle.
Thus, the sociologist is concerned with the types of authority that
predominate in the military establishment and the linkages
between the various hierarchies of authority. Do the systems of
authority operate to reenforce each other or do they operate to
create organizational strains? How appropriate is the actual

hierarchy of authority for the tasks and goals of the organization?

The Skill Structure

One approach to understanding the sources of organizational authority is to analyze the division of labor—the skill structure—in the military establishment. It is revealing to contrast the complex skill structure of a modern professional military organization—either under democratic or totalitarian political control—with the simple division of labor of the feudal armed force.[1] We can speak of the feudal or aristocratic type of military establishment as a composite model of Western European military organization before industrialism began to have its full impact. Survivals of these forms have persisted in most military establishments during the twentieth century.

The most striking aspect of the skill structure of the aristocratic military establishment is its close articulation with the then existing larger society. The military division of labor was simple, the levels of hierarchy few as well as rigidly defined, and within each stratum, specialization was almost nonexistent. The skill requirements were directly available in feudal society without additional specialized training. In particular, the aristocracy—the landed nobility—supplied the bulk of the necessary leadership, since their way of life prepared them for the requirements of warfare. Both family connection and common ideology ensured that military officers would form a cohesive group and would embody the ideology of the dominant groups in the social structure. Officership was not a specialized profession, but merely a part-time and occasional aspect of aristocratic existence. The officer even supplied his own weapons. The rank-and-file cadres were also drawn directly from their peacetime pursuits. Aside from small bands of mercenaries, soldiers came from the lower social strata where the appropriate skills for the few auxiliary weapons could be found. The role of warrior was a most honorable one and military status determined a person's prestige.

Because of the simple skill structure and relatively static organization, military authority was derived from tradition, custom, and social position. The aristocratic military establishment had an *ascriptive* system of authority. Authority was ascribed, in that persons were born into the officer class or they were excluded. Seldom could they earn such position through personal performance. The system of strict seniority, requiring promotion on the basis of age, is a keystone in the persistence of ascribed authority in modern armed forces. Age and length of service, like social status at birth, are ascribed group characteristics rather than marks of performance. The transforming of the aristocratic feudal military establishment into a professional armed force is linked to the growth of industrialism and the technological development of war. The traditional ascriptive basis of military authority becomes modified with a greater and greater reliance on criteria of *achievement* as the basis for allocating positions of authority. Performance in training, technical competence, and career records of the persons supplant birth, social connections, and inherited social status. The emergence of a professional army—that is, more specifically, a professional officer corps—was a slow and gradual transition with many interruptions and reversals. Although in the eighteenth century the signs were clearly discernible, one cannot speak of the emergence of a military profession until after 1800.

Law and medicine are identified as the more ancient professions. The professional practitioners, as a result of prolonged and specialized training, acquired a technique that enabled them to render a specialized service. But a professional group is more than a group with a special skill acquired through training. A professional group develops a sense of group identity and a complex of organizations for internal administration. Self-administration—often supported by state intervention—implies the growth of a body of ethics and a code of practice.[2] Samuel Huntington speaks of three essential elements in professionalism in the military: expertise, responsibility, and corporateness.[3]

The import of ethics and responsibility in the professionalization of the military is a complex and murky topic about which agreement is yet to be reached. But professionalism clearly means the emergence of a career service and the decline of the gentleman in warfare.[4] The aristocratic officer began to be displaced as artillery and more elaborate logistical planning required that the military be a trained and a full-time occupation. An upper-class education failed to provide the mathematical and engineering background that the occupation now required. Historical research highlights the evolution of the military profession as middle-class technicians during the nineteenth century took over the specialized artillery and engineering services, while the infantry and to an even greater extent the cavalry remained the domain of the aristocracy.[5] As the simple division of labor gave way to a complex pattern of specialization, the number of ranks increased and the staff officer emerged as a specialist in planning and coordination. The military became a profession in the employ of the state, separated by training from other professionals and dependent on the state for his complex instruments of warfare. All of these transformations implied that positions of authority would have to be allocated to persons with demonstrated competence, that is, on the basis of achievement.

In all types of organizations the dilemma of ascriptive versus achievement authority is ever present But it is a recurrent civilian perspective that the military establishment underemphasizes achievement in order to maintain traditional forms and the privileges of seniority. Thus, for example, the close link between age and rank in the military profession, particularly in naval organization, sets narrow limits within which skill is accorded positions of authority. In short, the hierarchical features of the military establishment strengthen the ascriptive sources of authority and compound the tasks of incorporating new skill groups.

First, there exists a deep source of organizational strain in all three services—ground, air, and naval—because the military staff-command structure does not articulate with its skill structure. In all three services the increased number and complexity of technical roles and specialists operate under the formally prescribed lines of authority developed for the simpler units of the past century. The basic dilemma centers about the staff officer, who despite his expanded functions and specialized skills, is defined as being subservient to the commanding officer. Originally, the role of the staff officer was defined as that of adviser to the commanding officer. Authority was vested solely in the commander. The supremacy of the commander appeared essential in order that specialists may operate within their competence and that they be effectively coordinated. This type of organizational structure in which the staff officer is limited to the role of adviser may have worked adequately as long as the technology of warfare developed slowly, but it presents continuing strain, given current complex technology.

As the division of labor becomes more complex and more specialized, the commander's dilemma becomes more pressing. He is not equipped with sufficient technical knowledge to supervise or assess adequately the performance of his technical subordinates. Nevertheless, the commander is held responsible for their performance by the formal hierarchy and the formal rules of the organization. The military establishment seeks to prepare him for this dilemma by increased schooling, by rotational assignments, and by specialized instruction in the techniques of administration.

Yet the military commander is forced to increase his reliance on staff officers to ensure that technical functions are efficiently performed in his own units and at lower echelons under his responsibility. The technical complexities of command force the commander to use his staff officers in supervisory as well as advisory roles. Authority conflicts are created for: (a) the staff officer charged with "producing" efficient performance of those lower-echelon functions falling within his technical competence, and (b) for the commander in the lower-echelon units under such supervision. If the staff officer, in his capacity as technical specialist (and employing his achieved authority), attempts to exercise authority over a technical function in a lower echelon, he is vulnerable to the allegation that he is using authority which is specifically denied him by the formal rules of the military establishment. But if he fails to exercise his supervisory control, he risks the charge of failing to assist his commander in executing his responsibilities. If the lower-echelon commander permits direct intervention for efficiency, he does so in the face of formal regulations. He thereby weakens his ascribed authority over his unit, and often his own staff officers refuse to act on the "suggestion" of the higher-staff officer. But if he resists direct higher-staff intervention, he is confronted with the reality that higher-echelon commanders may not share his emphasis on formal regulations. Or by preventing higher staff from exercising technical authority, he is forced to exercise supervision himself, although often he lacks the technical competence for this supervision.

In a highly suggestive study of organizational strains, Samuel Stouffer, Andrew Henry, and Edgar Borgatta investigated the attitudes toward staff-command relations in the United States Air Force.[6] They charted the opinions of 2,500 Air Force officers on the conditions under which they believed that a higher-echelon staff officer should handle a problem "unofficially" in a lower-echelon staff section through the staff channel—by dealing directly with the lower-level staff officer—as contrasted with the approved approach of handling it through command channels.

The extent to which reliance on informal channels is an acceptable norm is revealed by the fact that an overwhelming majority (77 per cent) of the officers favored direct staff intervention in a maintenance or supply problem occurring for the first time. In short, in the normal course of events, informal and unofficial staff intervention would be used. Moreover, when the same problem (maintenance and supply) has arisen frequently, 35 per cent still felt that such staff channels should be utilized. A stronger test of the reliance on such practices was officer opinion concerning a problem which was described as "seriously affecting the primary mission." For so serious a problem, 31 per cent still contended that they would use staff channels if the problem occurred for the first time. The die-hard "out of channels" officer drops to a very small minority of 15 per cent, who would use staff channels if the problem is seriously affecting the mission and has already come up in the lower-staff echelon several times. As would be expected, regular officers were least disposed to report that they would use staff channels, the volunteer reserve officer more disposed, and the involuntary reserve officer the most disposed. However, the magnitude of these differences was not striking, indicating that the staff-command dilemma operates for all types of officer personnel and reflects the basic problem of a complex skill structure operating within the formal military hierarchy.

Second, in the military establishment organizational strains exist which center about the continuous effort to develop a hierarchy of ranks appropriate to the new complex skill structure. In theory, in tradition, and in image the military rank system is a continuous pyramid with direct and clear-cut lines of authority and command channels from the top to the very bottom. In actuality, it has been transformed into a diamond-shaped hierarchy.

When armies became mass organizations through the introduction of the rifle, the assumption developed that a rank distribution of a single broadly based pyramid was the appropriate hierarchical form. The greatest number of men were privates, all of whom performed a relatively standardized task—infantrymen directly engaging the enemy. The task of the infantryman required only limited specialization, but it was a specialization without transferable skill to civilian employment. The officer of the line with his specialized training likewise had limited employment opportunities in the larger society. The number of officers at the higher levels of command and coordination dropped off progressively and sharply, but the concentration of technical specialists increased. In such a hierarchy the number of ranks could be small and the lines of authority could extend directly from the top to the very bottom. Traditionally, the Navy had a similar rank system.

However, the new skill structure of the military establishment is one in which specialization penetrates down the hierarchy into the formations assigned to combat. The concentration of persons engaged in purely military occupations is now a minority and even the combat occupations involve technical specialization The transferability of skill to civilian occupations is extremely widespread. Top-ranking generals and admirals particularly have many nonmilitary functions to perform which involve general managerial skills. These long-term changes in the military establishment can be seen from an occupational analysis of enlisted personnel since the Civil War. Military type of occupations accounted for 93.2 per cent of the personnel in the Civil War, but after the Spanish-American War the civilian type of occupations began to predominate. By 1954 only 28.8 per cent of Army personnel were engaged in purely military occupations. The percentages are undoubtedly lower for both Navy and Air Force personnel.

OCCUPATIONAL SPECIALIZATION IN ARMY ENLISTED
PERSONNEL, CIVIL WAR TO 1954

Occupational group	Civil War	Spanish American War	World War I	World War II	Korean War	Year 1954
Civilian type						
Technical, scientific	0.2	0.5	3.7	10.1	10.7	14.5
Administrative, clerical	0.7	3.1	8.0	14.6	19.2	17.5
Skilled mechanics, maintenance, etc.	0.6	1.1	21.5	15.8	16.9	20.3
Service workers	2.4	6.5	12.5	9.7	11.5	10.4
Operative, laborers	2.9	2.2	20.2	13.6	8.6	8.4
Military type	93.2	86.6	34.1	36.2	33.1	28.8

SOURCE: *Report on Conditions of Military Service for the President's Commission on Veterans' Pensions*, Question IV (Nature of Military Duties), December 28, 1955.

As already indicated, to meet the organizational requirements of this proliferation of skills, the military hierarchy has had to be adjusted, so that the allocation of ranks is no longer a pyramid, but is closer to a diamond in shape. More accurately, two diamond-shaped hierarchies—one for the enlisted men and one for the officers corps—have emerged. For example, the distribution of enlisted grades in a typical bomb squadron was reported at the end of the Korean hostilities as:[7]

	Per cent
Master sergeants	7.0
Technical sergeants	10.3
Staff sergeants	15.2
Airmen first class	24.4
Airmen second class	28.1
Airmen third class	13.5
Basic airmen	1.5
Total	100.0

The diamond shape is even more marked in certain technical and maintenance units. So also, the Personnel Act of 1947, which sought 51,000 active duty officers for the ground forces, made captain the most prevalent rank, with the number of second lieutenants approximately equal to that of majors.

This changed pattern of rank gives the impression of an inflation in rank. An infantry regiment in 1939 had three master sergeants, while in 1955 a single infantry company had five. In 1939 the infantry squad leader was a corporal; in 1956 he was a sergeant first class. In part, this development is a response to the need to raise the status and income of the soldier. In part, it is also a tendency of organizations to grow internally. But basically, this expansion of the middle strata of ranks—officers and enlisted men—is a typical manifestation of organizations which have grown more complex and where achievement criteria weigh heavily in the allocation of authority.

This proliferation of the middle-officer ranks also creates the image of a weakening of authority, since officers hold their rank not merely on the basis of the number of subordinates they command but because of their technical skills. In reality, authority has not been so much weakened as transformed. The tasks of military authority now more often relate to lateral coordination and cooperation than to the exercise of responsibility of the highest echelons over the lowest echelons. The task of the highest echelons is to create the conditions for the middle strata of specialists to coordinate their efforts. Consider a typical operation in the Korean conflict where an infantry combat team required air support from carrier-based planes, and it is abundantly clear that direct orders of a hierarchical variety are being supplemented by complex lateral coordination.

Military leadership is continuously seeking to offset the apparent weakening of authority by attempting to create a separate hierarchy of technical specialists and a separate hierarchy of commanders. The object is to reestablish something approaching a pyramid type of structure with clear lines of authority from the top to the very bottom. But fundamentally the new skill structure does not permit or allow for so simple a hierarchy. As the military establishment becomes more enmeshed in engineering and development, it is more difficult to maintain the distinction between the commander and the technical specialist. In the Air Force, which is an organization of combat flyers and former combat flyers, the organizational crisis is the deepest, since displacement of the "fighter" is proceeding more rapidly and more completely than in the ground or naval forces.

Traditional hierarchical authority is the basis on which the military establishment maintains its organizational boundaries. Such authority comes to be shared with the authority of skill and achievement, despite formal channels of command and the official hierarchy of rank.

Status Systems

Sociological analysis has long recognized that status systems are required to regulate and control the tensions and conflicts generated by competition among differing systems of authority. Authority, ascribed or achieved, is not operative because of the ultimate sanctions that an officer can mobilize. Rather, in any organization, civilian or military, authority systems operate on a day-to-day basis or fail to operate because of the status—that is, the prestige and the respect—the officers have. If authority is traditional and ascribed, status systems are likely to be fixed and clear-cut. But with the extension of achievement and skill criteria for allocating authority, status systems become fluid and are not clear-cut. Skilled specialists or men with outstanding combat records, despite low rank, may be accorded higher prestige than officers with higher rank. When status and prestige are in sharp variation to the contributions a person renders to an organization, authority systems are certain to be subject to strain and tension.

The effectiveness of military authority is deeply conditioned by the status and prestige which civilian society accords the military profession. It is generally recognized that, despite public acclaim of individual military heroes, officership is a low-status profession. The results of a national sampling of opinion placed the prestige of the officer in the armed services not only below the physician, scientist, college professor, and minister, but even below that of the public schoolteacher.[8] In this study, the relative prestige of the Air Force and Navy was above that of the Army and the Marine Corps, as measured by adult opinion as to which service they preferred for their sons. Yet one adult civilian in two felt that he would be pleased if his son took up a career in the military services. Interestingly enough, the less educated civilian holds both the military officer and the public servant in higher esteem than does the better educated.[9]

An adequate level of prestige, difficult though that may be to define, is required to maintain organizational effectiveness and to inhibit excessive personnel turnover. In addition, the relatively low prestige of the military in the eyes of civilians conditions the conception that the military profession holds of itself. The military takes over this civilian image, with the result that the military exhibits extreme status sensitivity. The concern with status of the military professional is to be traced not only to the hierarchical organization of the armed forces. The military behaves very much like any other minority or low-status group.

It is, therefore, not surprising that the military establishment has evolved an elaborate basis for according its limited supply of status and prestige to its own members. Most pervasive is the criterion which is applied universally through the services, the distinction between the officers and the enlisted men. The other universal distinctions are between regulars and reservists, line versus staff, combat versus noncombat, and the like. There are also more particular designations, such as veteran status of a particular campaign, membership in a high-status formation, or graduation from a service academy.

An effort was made by a University of North Carolina Air Force research group to study empirically status rivalries at selected Air Force bases.[10] On the whole, these research studies were mainly descriptive and did not analyze in detail the consequences of status rivalries on organizational behavior. They overlooked the positive influences that status systems have on initiative and incentives. Two of the collaborators, James D. Thompson and Richard L. Simpson, summarized their orientation with the hypothesis that "when members of a minority status class are concentrated in certain parts of a unit, especially in positions of authority, organizational stress is likely to develop." Social scientists will be required to develop a more comprehensive view of the nature and consequences of status rivalries in military systems.

A published study from this project by Raymond Mack underlines the observation, well known to every alert military commander, that flying in the Air Force has more prestige than decision-making at the lower echelons; that is, operational units outrank command units in prestige.[11] But this system of prestige does not extend throughout the entire hierarchy. Although a combat ideology pervades the highest echelons, the prestige of decision-making and planning increases, the higher the officer advances. Thus, in their career development Air Force officers and officers in the other services must readjust their perspectives, often with great difficulty, to new professional requirements.

Changing Military Discipline

The new skill structure modifies military discipline as well as status. At first glance, the military establishment is a vast organization for technical and logistical operations and a preponderance of its personnel are engaged in administrative and housekeeping functions. But military authority, if it is to be effective, must strive to make combat units its organizational prototype, and the character of military organization can best be seen in combat units. In combat the maintenance of initiative has become a requirement of greater importance than the rigid enforcement of discipline. In the succinct formulation of S. L. A. Marshall, "The philosophy of discipline has adjusted to changing conditions. As more and more impact has gone into the hitting power of weapons, necessitating ever-widening deployments in the forces of battle, the quality of the initiative in the individual has become the most praised of the military virtues."[12]

In a sense, the military ideology of authoritarian discipline has always been tempered by the necessities of human nature. But the close order formations based on relatively low firepower could be dominated and controlled by direct and rigid discipline. However, since the development of the rifle bullet of more than a century ago, the social organization of combat units has been changing continuously so as to throw the individual fighter on his own and his primary group's resources. Despite the proliferation of military technology, all three services are dependent on the initiative of a very small percentage of the fighting personnel, who are willing to press the attack under all circumstances. The Air Force discovered that less than one per cent of its military pilots became aces—five victories in air battle; yet this one per cent accounted roughly for 30 to 40 per cent of the enemy aircraft destroyed in the air.

In World War II and again in the Korean conflict, the command problem in the ground forces centered on developing the ability of the infantry soldier to make the fullest use of his weapons. The infantry squad, the air crew, and the submarine complement, all have wide latitude for making decisions requiring energy and initiative. The increased firepower of modern weapons causes military forces—land, sea, and air—to be more dispersed, in order to reduce exposure to danger. Each unit becomes increasingly dependent on its own organizational impetus, once the battle has started. Thus, the military establishment with its hierarchical structure, with its exacting requirements for coordination, and with its apparently high centralization of organizational power, must strive contrariwise to develop the broadest decentralization of initiative at the point of contact with the enemy. As the destructiveness of weapons systems increases, short of total destruction, the importance of initiative increases for the military formations that survive the initial exchange of hostilities.

The combat soldier, regardless of military arm, when committed to battle, is hardly the model of Max Weber's ideal bureaucrat following rigid rules and regulations. In certain respects he is the antithesis. The combat fighter is not routinized and self-contained. Rather, his role is one of constant improvisation, regardless of his service or weapon. Improvisation is the keynote of the individual fighter or combat group. The impact of battle destroys men, equipment, and organization that need constantly to be brought back into some form of unity through on-the-spot improvisation. In battle the planned division of labor breaks down.

The technology of warfare is so complex that the coordination of a group of specialists cannot be guaranteed simply by authoritarian discipline. Members of a military group recognize their greater mutual dependence on the technical proficiency of their team members than on the formal authority structure. The military organization dedicated to victory is forced to alter its techniques of training and indoctrination. Rather than developing automatic reaction to combat dangers, it requires a training program designed to teach men not only to count on instruction from superiors but also to exercise their own judgment about the best response to make when confronted with given types of danger. The very designation "combat team" exemplifies the goals of such indoctrination, since it emphasizes the positive contributions of each person regardless of rank. Thus, the operational code of the Israeli forces in the Sinai campaign was, in effect, "when in doubt, attack"—an expression of sheer initiative.

Obviously, technology conditions these changing internal social relations in the military establishment. The morale and coordination of a complex group of specialists cannot be guaranteed simply by authoritarian discipline. The complexity of the machinery and the resultant social interdependence produce an important residue of organizational power for each participating member. All the members of a military group recognize their mutual dependence on the technical proficiency and level of performance of others, as well as on the formal authority structure.

Thus, the impact of technology has forced a shift in the practices of military authority. Military authority must shift from reliance on practices based on *domination* to a wider utilization of *manipulation*. Traditional or ascriptive authority relies heavily on domination, while manipulation is more appropriate for authority based on achievement. By domination we mean influencing a person's behavior, by giving explicit instruction as to desired behavior without reference to the goals sought. Domination involves threats and negative sanctions rather than positive incentives. It tends to produce mechanical compliance. Manipulation involves influencing an individual's behavior less by giving explicit instructions and more by indirect techniques of group persuasion and by an emphasis on group goals. While the term "manipulation" has come to be thought of as morally reprehensible, it describes the efforts of leadership when orders are issued and the reasons for them are given. It is impossible to analyze modern institutions without reference to a concept such as manipulation, or some more socially acceptable equivalent. Manipulation involves positive incentives rather than physical threats; manipulation does retain the threat of exclusion from the group as a control. The indirect techniques of manipulation are designed to take into account the individual soldier's predispositions.

The goal of military authority, in ideal terms, is to create stable and purposeful involvement at each level in the hierarchy of ranks. When military leaders operate successfully, they make use of their organizational skills to produce effective participation. So it can be said, as older forms of domination become outmoded, effective participation becomes a new criterion for judging military authority. There is no clear-cut conceptual agreement even in idealized terms about the nature of such authority, but the problem is crucial for all types of hierarchical organization. Terms such as "participant authority" and "fraternal authority" have been offered, but the specific designation is not the basic issue. It is, however, necessary to keep in mind that use of the term "democratic authority" by some social psychologists is both unfortunate and misleading. Democratic authority applies political processes especially to election contests and serves little purpose in analyzing administrative and organizational behavior, especially military organization.

The military establishment, despite its hierarchical structure and legal code, presents a striking case of this shift from domination to increased reliance on manipulation. There are cyclical trends in military discipline but the important issue is that the shift toward manipulation has been gradual and long term. The development of an operating doctrine to accommodate the military profession in the United States to these requirements started before World War I, but it was not until World War II that these trends were directly acknowledged. The transformation of military authority can be seen in every phase of organizational behavior—for example, the narrowing of the differences in privileges, status, and even uniforms of the enlisted man and the officer, the development of conference techniques of command from the smallest unit to the Joint Chiefs of Staff themselves, or the rewriting of military law into the new Uniform Code. Emphasis on manipulative control varies as between the services, depending on the rate and nature of technological change. The Air Force in some respects has gone the farthest in modification of its organizational behavior.

Yet the long-term outcome of the current transformation from an emphasis on domination to increased reliance on manipulation is problematic. It is abundantly clear that present forms are highly transitional. Since the shift in function of military authority is based on organizational requirements, it is not surprising that even armies of totalitarian political systems display these same features. The organizational effectiveness of the Wehrmacht was based on well-developed practices of manipulation and group cohesion, within the context of radical repression of extreme political and ideological deviation.

Indeed, the shift away from organizational discipline based on domination is a manifestation of all types of modern large-scale bureaucracies. However, because of the severity and uncertain nature of combat, the military has been forced to react more dramatically and extensively to the pressures for indirect rule. Since the new discipline must operate within a hierarchical structure and must serve the need for complicated coordinating mechanisms, the shift from domination to manipulation develops high levels of organizational strain and many unsolved dilemmas.

The contradictory interplay of practices designed to stimulate group initiative and those practices required for organizational coordination are again widespread contemporary bureaucratic processes. It can be argued that they are more extreme in military than in civilian organizations. Organizations can and do function effectively despite internal strain and dilemmas. But the military organization has special characteristics which complicate and disrupt the successful incorporation of authority based on indirect control, group decision, and other manipulative techniques.

Devices for maintaining organization balance under conflicting requirements are slow to develop. Thus, for example, extensive training and expertise are required to develop an officer cadre skilled in applying indirect techniques of control, whose use of indirect techniques of leadership will be accepted by subordinates as valid and not merely as a sham. The gap between formal regulation and procedures and the informal realities of command is also especially great. This becomes a source of tension and confusion, since it is obvious and easily criticized. The wide difference between the official and the unofficial is perpetuated, since the realities of combat are passed on from one generation to the next by personal contacts, or informally, and not officially or explicitly.

Equally disruptive to orderly incorporation of indirect discipline is the ideological orientation of portions of the military elite. In the United States and elsewhere, the military elite holds a basic conservative ideological and political orientation and often is alarmed at, and misinterprets, the new requirements of military authority.[13] Segments of the military elite see the new requirements as potentially undermining the entire basis of authority and coordination and as barriers to decisions on the strategic level. Concern with technological change does not necessarily imply concern with organizational change. Such officers fail to see how manipulative techniques supply the basis for developing the necessary strong subleadership required to operate effectively within a well-managed and closely supervised military formation. In fact, they fail to see that indirect and manipulative control of a rank-and-file leadership based on positive group cohesion is essential to maintain both decentralized initiative and operational control over widely dispersed military formations. The "bruderschaft" of the Waffen SS represents an example of how such procedures can be developed within a very rigid command structure.

It is not necessary to assume that indirect social control implies an inability to arrive at strategic or tactical decisions. To the contrary, staff work in support of the strategic commander has traditionally assumed a range of interplay before the responsible authority arrives at a decision. The requirements of command have pushed this form of decision-making down to the lowest operational units. It is understandable that such a trend is resisted by military traditionalists. Military elites, typically, are concerned that indirect control should not undermine the basic authority structure and, therefore, feel repeatedly compelled, without clear criteria, to attempt to limit the use of group consensus procedures by lower commanders. Consequently, as the older techniques of military domination break down under technological requirements, newer forms based on manipulation emerge as highly unstable and loaded with tension. One formulation of the research task of sociologists is to study the strength versus the organizational vulnerability of contemporary military discipline. A functional analysis of changing military discipline requires an examination of at least three topics, which comprise the subject matter of the next chapters: the assimilation of military roles, primary group structure, and techniques of organizational control.

NOTES TO CHAPTER II

[1] Vagts, Alfred, *A History of Militarism*. W. W. Norton and Co., New York, 1937.

[2] Carr-Saunders, A. M., and P. A. Wilson, *The Professions*, Clarendon Press, Oxford, England, 1933; Henderson, L. J., "Physician and Patient as a Social System," *New England Journal of Medicine*, vol. 212, 1935, pp. 816–823; Parsons, Talcott, "The Professions and Social Structure," Chapter 8 of *Essays in Sociological Theory, Pure and Applied*, The Free Press, Glencoe, Ill., 1949.

[3] Huntington, Samuel P., *The Soldier and the State*. Harvard University Press, Cambridge, Mass., 1957, pp. 7–10.

[4] Michael A. Lewis in his *England's Sea-Officers:* The Story of the Naval Profession, Allen and Unwin, Ltd., London, 1939, traces the historical development of the British naval officer. The author defines professionalism in the military exclusively in terms of career considerations: provisions for the con-

tinuous entry of young officers, system of training the young officer, regular employment of the trained officer, reasonable chances of the officer rising gradually in professional, financial, and social status, steady exodus at the upper end of the service, retirement.

⁵ Demeter, Karl, *Das Deutsche Heer und Seine Offiziere*. Verlag von Reimar Hobbing, Berlin, 1935.

⁶ This study by Samuel A. Stouffer, Andrew F. Henry, and Edgar F. Borgatta is an example of a military service, the U. S. Air Force, creating the conditions for a social scientific investigation of a basic aspect of its organizational behavior. The portions of this study dealing with staff-command role dilemma have not been published. The findings are available in Final Report of Contract AF33 (038)—12782—Staff Command conflicts and other sources of tension in relation to officer leadership and organizational effectiveness.

⁷ Mack, Raymond W., *Social Stratification on U.S. Air Force Bases*. Technical Report no. 4, Air Force Base Project, Institute for Research in Social Science, University of North Carolina, Chapel Hill, undated, p. 10.

⁸ Public Opinion Surveys, Inc., Princeton, N. J., *Attitudes of Adult Civilians Toward the Military Services as a Career*. Prepared for the Office of Armed Forces Information and Education, Department of Defense, Washington, 1955.

⁹ Janowitz, Morris, and Deil S. Wright, "The Prestige of Public Employment," *Public Administration Review*, vol. 16, Winter, 1956, pp. 15–21.

¹⁰ Air Force Base Project. Sponsored by Human Resources Research Institute, U.S. Air Force, and executed by the Institute for Research in Social Science, University of North Carolina, Chapel Hill. See in particular, Mack, Raymond W., *op. cit.;* and Thompson, James D., and Richard L. Simpson, *Status Classes, Morale, and Performance in the United States Air Force*, Technical Report no. 6, October, 1952.

¹¹ Mack, Raymond W., "The Prestige System of an Air Base: Squadron Rankings and Morale," *American Sociological Review*, vol. 19, June, 1954, pp. 281–287.

¹² Marshall, S. L. A., *Men Against Fire*. William Morrow and Co., New York, 1947, p. 22.

¹³ Brown, C. S., *The Social Attitudes of American Generals, 1898–1940*. Unpublished doctoral dissertation, University of Wisconsin, Madison, Wis., 1951.

III

ASSIMILATION OF MILITARY ROLES

Few organizations place as much emphasis on procedures for assimilating new members as does the military establishment. Assimilation involves the ongoing process of recruitment, selection, training, and career development. Not only must the new recruit, officer, or enlisted man learn a complex of technical skills. He is also expected to master an elaborate code of social behavior and professional honor, since membership in the military means participation in an organizational community which regulates behavior both on and off the "job." In the process of assimilation the recruit learns the roles, the required behaviors of his office, which he must perform regardless of his personal preferences. Whatever gratification and rewards military life may offer, military occupations are frequently hazardous, strenuous, and at times irksome. Assimilation of military roles requires strong positive motives if military tasks are to be performed with dispatch.

Since the specific tasks of the armed forces are constantly changing under the impact of technology, assimilation literally extends throughout the entire career of the professional soldier. Career advancement also means abandoning one type of military role—tactical combat—for another, organizational leadership and command. This is a difficult process involving extensive retraining. In a period in which the military establishment is directed to deter total thermonuclear war, and yet the possibility of limited warfare is in the forefront of international relations, it is not an exaggeration to speak of the crisis in the mechanics of assimilating military roles. Personnel has to be recruited and trained for multiple roles and for roles about which there is neither agreement nor clarity. For a long time sociologists have been concerned with the mechanics of assimilation, since it is through these processes that organizations demonstrate their viability. The sociological perspective toward the assimilation of new roles in the military highlights the continuity of a person's social behavior before and after initiation into the organization.

The military behavior of the selectee in World War II or in the Korean conflict was just as much a function of his conditioning in civilian life as it was a result of the military training he received. Changes in military life and changes in the society from which the officer and the enlisted personnel come are closely linked. The professional soldier and the civilian soldier are both products of the same social system. It is a fundamental error to assume that the military establishment is some sort of self-contained organism which digests and assimilates foreign bodies. Such an image implies that the military is a vestigial appendage rather than an organ of contemporary society. The sociological perspective does not deny the unique characteristics of the military establishment, nor does it overlook the respects in which the military may lag behind civilian society.

It does, however, affirm that the orientation which the civilian society gives to recruits—officers and enlisted men—will either assist or retard their assimilation of military roles. It affirms also that the professional cadres who have the responsibility of training new personnel have a definition of their job which comes from the basic values of civilian society.

Recruitment

What are the social dimensions of civilian life which assist or hinder recruits in assimilating military roles? Obviously, civilian orientations toward military service vary, depending upon whether recruitment is for a peacetime or a wartime establishment. In the continuing "cold war" period, the military is confronted with the difficulties of recruiting for an establishment which is neither peacetime nor wartime in the traditional sense. Currently, the selective service system is required to maintain the personnel requirements of the ground forces, while the naval and air formations are based on professionals, as well as limited term volunteers and reservists, many of whom are responding to the pressures of selective service.

Pacifism, religious or political, is hardly widespread in the United States although it may be growing. Military service is accepted because of recognized necessities. But for the potential recruit, especially the volunteer, a positive attitude is based not only on the task of the armed forces but also on the fact that the military offers an adequate and respectable level of personal security. For the enlisted man seeking a professional career, it offers relatively promising possibilities. The strong regulations requiring nondiscriminatory practices—whether they be regional or racial-ethnic, or social class—have had the consequence of attracting the socially disadvantaged, especially lower-class persons with rural backgrounds, and Negroes who develop strong career commitments to the services. De Tocqueville already saw that for many enlisted men military life was an avenue for social advancement in a manner similar to particular civilian occupations.[1] For the potential professional officer not only does the military profession offer an opportunity for education and social mobility, but it is generally considered to be an occupation which stands in contrast to the many routine tasks of civilian life. It is a profession with a sense of mission and adventuresome experiences, especially those connected with travel.

The raising of the pay scale of the armed forces in 1958, as a result of the Cordiner Committee Report, was designed to enhance career opportunities in the military and thereby decrease personnel turnover. In the new pay scale there is a sharp weakening of the traditional principles of pay increases based on length of service and an effort to develop rewards on the basis of merit. It is doubtful whether the military profession, as a profession, can solve its personnel problems on the basis of incentive pay scales, important as this may be. In the long run the rewards of civilian industry are likely to be more attractive for the most highly skilled and most proficient. The attraction of the military service for the professional involves such factors as style of life, social status, sense of mission, and the importance of military honor.

By sharp contrast the negative image of the military establishment in the American social structure stands as a powerful barrier to the recruitment of personnel. In a society in which indi-
vidualism and personal gain are paramount virtues, it is understandable that wide sectors of the civilian population view the
military career as a weak choice, as an effort to "sell out" cheaply
for economic security and low pay and limited prestige. In this
view the free enterprise system is real and hard, so that the persons who are weak and unable to withstand the rigors of competition seek escape into the military. Repeatedly, this observation
has been made with particular reference to the enlisted personnel
in the peacetime establishment. "In the regular army . . . the
majority of the enlisted men are concerned with individual
security rather than with competitive achievement."[2] It is difficult to explain why the military establishment, which is an
organization founded on the function of violence, which places a
high evaluation upon masculinity and aggressiveness, and which,
in effect, has many elements of career insecurity, should be
selected by personalities seeking to "escape" the realities of
civilian life.

It is indeed paradoxical that the military should be envisaged
as offering a safer refuge than most civilian occupations. For a
peacetime military of the pre-1939 type, this "escapist" career
motivation may have been more relevant an explanation. In any
case, the type of personality which seeks excessively to "prove"
his masculinity in the military environment is represented by the
"neurotic" recruit whose military behavior under stress is most
likely to be highly unsatisfactory.[3] Or, as the authors of *The
American Soldier* conclude, "Broadly, we can say that the evidence
seems to show that a stable home background, a healthy child-
hood, good work habits in school and association with other boys
and girls, including participation in sports, were assets for the young
civilian who put on the uniform and tried to adjust to Army life."
They believe that these characteristics might be held to be typical
of "good" rather than "poor" adjustment to civilian society. On
the other hand, they were negatively associated with the probability of going AWOL and with psychoneurotic breakdown.[4]

While it can be argued that the military services do not attract disproportionate concentrations of persons maladjusted to civilian occupational opportunities, such persons may still be pressured into military service by the civilian community as a kind of preparatory school for life, for "making a man" out of a recruit. In fact, many of the aspects of military life which are deprecated by civilian sentiments can at the same time be pointed to as reasons why civilian society believes the military can operate as a reformatory. The military establishment is an all-male culture which informally tolerates behavioral excesses to a greater degree than does mixed civilian society. The military provides a disciplined and predictable environment in which persons not able to utilize the freedom of civilian society can more readily adjust. The need for conformity in the military establishment is put forth in the interest of national security and in these terms can be more readily internalized.

As a result, young adolescents in the throes of intergenerational conflict and students without clear-cut goals are advised to join the services and "grow up." Near delinquents are often encouraged to join or are "paroled" into the armed forces. It is noteworthy that the armed forces are able to help certain of these deviant youths. Precise evidence exists that felons who were paroled to the armed forces during wartime had a much lower recidivism rate than those paroled to civilian life.[5]

In time of war and during the contemporary cold war, conscription has been necessary to meet manpower requirements. Another fundamental barrier to the assimilation of recruits to the armed forces is the ambiguous perspective of American society toward distributing the risks of universal military training. Again, the issue is not opposition in civilian society to institutionalized violence or to aggressive behavior. Rather, it is that selective service produces the same traditional negativism and opposition to governmental authority which has so deeply characterized United States historical development.

The efficacy of the selective service system assumes public sentiments which insist on an equal distribution of risks. At the outbreak of World War II, public opinion in the United States was not characterized by hysterical pressure against "draft dodgers." In contrast to World War I, there were few counterparts to the white feathers, the painting of homes yellow, and the use of the epithet "slacker." Instead, there was a widespread acceptance of the decisions of selective service and the feeling that those not in uniform had sufficient reasons. Universal service was accepted as essential and the importance of an organized allocation of manpower was taken for granted. At the same time, the national community sanctioned personal efforts to influence and determine one's own fate under selective service, if these efforts were justified and within the meaning of the law.

After two decades of selective service, civilian perspectives no longer operate to assist assimilation of recruits into the armed forces. Overt opposition to the system, even political criticism of its injustices, is virtually absent. But even in the absence of adequate empirical studies, it is clear that there is widespread confusion about military manpower systems, deprecation of the administration of these programs, and a reluctance to serve. Already by May, 1952, during the Korean War, 83 per cent of a cross-section sample of 2,975 university students were found by Cornell University social scientists to be essentially negative toward their military service obligations.[6]

In the cold war one can point out that when war is reduced to a potentiality rather than an immediate actuality, such perspectives are very likely to develop. Since the potential selectee tends to evaluate the threat to national security as one involving total war, he finds it difficult to believe that his limited personal contribution is of any relevance. Those who have served in the cold war army, while they may understand the relevance of basic training, report to their civilian contacts that after basic training most of their military experience seemed without point.

But from the point of view of military management, the issue is deeper. The reluctance to perform military service is a fundamental expression of the personal hedonism of contemporary society. The Cornell University study found that personal, rather than military or ideological, factors were at the root of negative attitudes toward being called into the military forces. These personal factors included disruption of plans, influence of friends and family, and feelings of relative deprivation.

The administration of the selective service system has come to condition perspectives in those who are selected, which handicap the military establishment. Few selectees believe that the system works to allocate manpower in a rational or just way. The pattern of deferments and exemptions, particularly for married men with dependents, and the fact that only a very small proportion of each age group actually serves, are the basis for this resentment. Although not necessarily outspoken or articulate in criticism of the selective service procedures, many of these youths, who see no basis for their selection, develop powerful negativism toward military authority, which complicates their assimilation. These negative attitudes can be so deep that selectees succeed in communicating their hostility to the professional cadres and, even adversely, influence the performance of junior officers.

Selection and Training

Assimilation into the military establishment rests on the assumption that scientific personnel selection is the first and perhaps basic step. The object of selection ought to be to locate personnel with potentials for combat and for combat leadership. In selecting for officer training, and especially for entrance into the service academies, the object ought to be to screen for potential strategic leadership.

After forty years of research and development in military personnel selection, it is abundantly clear that there exist no satisfactory and reliable techniques for accomplishing either task. Nevertheless, personnel selection is an essential and accepted aspect of military management, if only because it helps to eliminate some of the markedly unfit and because it is relevant in the selection of a variety of technical personnel. In part, the failure of personnel selection has been a theoretical one, because personnel psychologists have sought to identify specific individual leadership traits when it is clear that leadership involves an interaction between personality attributes and social situations.

In 1947 W. O. Jenkins in "A Review of Leadership Studies with Particular Reference to Military Problems," summarized the state of knowledge, as of the close of World War II.[7] He concludes that Morris Viteles' evaluation of leadership studies made in 1932 had not yet been modified. The record of accomplishment is not a brilliant one; no single trait or group of characteristics has been isolated, setting off the leader from the members of his group.

In a more recent summary which includes post World War II efforts, Fillmore H. Sanford reasserted the same conclusion:

> Much effort, both scientific and otherwise, has been invested in the attempt to select young men who will turn out to be good military leaders. It is fair to say that, in contrast to the obvious success scored in recent years in the selection of people for various kinds of specific jobs, no one has yet devised a method of proven validity for selecting either military or non-military leaders.[8]

These studies, especially as they focus on tactical military leadership, overlook the inescapable observations of combat commanders and combat observers. The gap between noncombat and combat is so great that the traits manifested by a person in a formal psychological test are a poor indicator of his performance under the excruciating stress of combat. Men who were "bad actors" in training, marked by faults of laziness, unruliness, and disorderliness, have become consistent leaders on the battlefield, with all of the virtues of sustained aggressiveness, obedience to higher command, and careful calculation. Those who could fight but who would not soldier are too well known, too prominent, and too important in the military to have escaped the observation of personnel testers. Since virtually all of these trait studies fail to seek validation in actual combat performance, their relevance is sharply limited. There is, however, one conclusion from these trait studies which is highly relevant. Repeatedly, it has been found that academic and scholastic achievements are unrelated to military leadership; this is neither a basis for selection nor for rejection.[9]

One study of combat infantry personnel in Korea, prepared under the auspices of the Human Resources Research Office, represents the most elaborate effort to discover the traits of soldiers that relate to performance in combat.[10] Among combat troops, fighters were distinguished from nonfighters on the basis of buddies' reports, as well as evidence based on self-reporting.

The results showed that factors such as better health and vitality, more intelligence, a great fund of military knowledge, and greater speed and accuracy on performance tests were found to be statistically more prevalent among fighters. These variables would characterize active leadership regardless of the task at hand. However, the striking conclusion is that the degree of association was not pronounced and, therefore, these variables were hardly the crucial ones. More fundamental from a theoretical point of view, the fighter was more masculine, more socially mature, had greater emotional stability and a more stable home life as compared with the nonfighter. Again, each factor by itself was hardly distinguishing in a crucial sense. However, if one thinks of the group requirements of combat, these traits become indices of a person's ability to participate in primary group organization under combat. Thus, for example, one of the most distinguishing characteristics was that the nonfighters came from homes in which the fathers had died before the son was eighteen years old. Such persons were deprived of the opportunity for identification with a male and for developing the capacity to participate in the all-male society of the military.

In contrast to this tradition of searching for leadership traits, there has been a growing emphasis on a more sociological group process approach to understanding selection and leadership recruitment. Leadership, in this view, does not adhere to the individual, but is a varying relationship between personality and social situation. While this approach has proved valuable in the development of criteria for eliminating unfit personnel, again there is no reason to believe that selection procedures based on group processes are dramatically more valid and important.

Clearly, mass psychiatric screening has become an indispensable tool of military management, since the psychiatric approach emphasizes probable reaction of leaders and followers under stress and in differing group situations. But psychiatric screening of the unfit has only slowly developed a sensitivity to the organizational requirements for which the screening is performed. During World War II the rate of rejection was unduly high, to the point of cutting down manpower reserves, because the goal was the unrealistic one of eliminating all men who might break down in military service. The process was aimed at the selection of veterans, not soldiers. Since all personnel have a psychiatric breaking point under stress, the standards have shifted to a concern with the elimination of the most unfit and to the possibility of proper assignment. Even more fundamental is the fact that there is considerable evidence that some neurotic types perform adequately and even well in the stress situation of military life, and it is difficult if not impossible to identify these in advance.[11]

The development of the group process approach to leadership selection received its impetus in the British army. The British had long resisted scientific selection, but after the crisis of Dunkerque, they faced the tasks of rationalizing their officer selection system and developed a program with great rapidity and thoroughness. The British selection system sought by quasi-experimental group situations to observe the behavior of men under stress and in leaderless situations in order to note which men would emerge as effective leaders.[12] Since these group experiments sought to reproduce some of the actual situations confronting tactical leadership, this approach is theoretically more relevant, although validation has not been extensive. These procedures were paralleled in the selection experiments of the Office of Strategic Services for its unconventional warfare operations. Unfortunately, the OSS research efforts, because they deal with such highly specialized personnel and because no attempts at validation were made, contributed little to the development of personnel selection in the U.S. armed forces.[13]

In general, this type of personnel selection has not fitted into the orientation of U.S. personnel selection experts. In part, this is an expression of an individual psychological orientation and a lack of concern for the analysis of group processes. It is also an expression of resistance to the cumbersome techniques involved in group testing which require judgmental decisions by the rating personnel. Instead, the group approach to personnel selection in the United States has centered around sociometric testing procedures, which, regardless of their validity, can be reduced to simple self-administered paper-and-pencil tests. These sociometric techniques for selecting leaders by nomination of peers, as well as by superiors, are usually built into training experiences. Although such studies often tend to be fragmentary, there is evidence that peers can predict with some accuracy those most likely to succeed in officer candidate school. Peer estimates may even be more accurate than those of superiors. However, there has been no sustained effort to validate sociometric leader selection in combat or combat-like situations. In fact, the sociometric approach is subject to the criticism that it reflects popularity rather than the crucial social relations required to sustain groups under stress. On the other hand, the sociometric perspective may be much more appropriate for assisting in understanding the social cohesion of combat units if the findings of sociometric tests are recast into a theoretical perspective. D. M. Goodacre has reported a field experiment in which a high correlation was found between group cohesion, as measured by reciprocated sociometric choices, and performance on a realistic scout problem.[14]

The classification and selection of specialists for particular technical jobs, and even the selection of combat aviators during World War II and subsequently, is a markedly different problem from that of generalized military leadership. Aviators were not selected primarily as leaders; they were selected as aviators. It has been clearly demonstrated that old-fashioned selection boards did not succeed better in predicting who would survive aviation training than could be accomplished by flipping coins, and that scientifically devised selection tests did succeed in making such predictions with a resulting increase in efficiency. The improved selection of aviators as aviators leaves unanswered the question of how to develop leadership potential among these men who have been selected for a specific technical task. What is needed is a broadening of interest in research away from selection as a device to an understanding of the process of assimilation into the military, which involves not only selection but also the dynamics of training and of career development.

Assimilation during initial training requires adapting the recruit to an all-male society and to a social organization committed to violence. At the most personal level the recruit faces a loss of privacy and exposure to a pervasive set of controls. While most personnel will ultimately perform logistical and administrative functions, the core of the training process centers around combat requirements.

Training new recruits for combat has in the past been governed by a conception of shock treatment—of the need for a sudden and decisive break with civilian life and rapid exposure to the rigors of military existence. The officer candidate had to receive a double dosage of shock treatment, since he had to be separated not only from civilian society but also from the enlisted ranks. The devices of shock range from the "beast barracks" of West Point for new cadets to the well-known Marine haircut. The sharp and sudden transition is often repulsive to the civilian orientation. But, in the military establishment, the assumption is that only a decisive break is effective in the long run and that the rigors of basic training are in effect natural techniques of selection.

The shock technique was an essential element of the older forms of discipline based on domination. It probably had some functional utility. But with the development of military organization based on group consensus, the training procedures have had to be modified. It is clearly impossible for highly technical arms to achieve group consensus on the basis of negative sanctions. Instead, new ideals of assimilation stress positive attachments and group loyalties. While the residues of shock treatment persist, military training has become a more gradual process of assimilation. It is more a process of fostering positive incentives and group loyalties through a team concept. The training cadres—officers and enlisted men—must establish their competence and their interest in their men, for they cannot rely merely on their ultimate military authority and sanctions.

Barriers to the development of functional training procedures are immense. The training cadres vary in their acceptance of new procedures and in their skills to implement them. Often large groups of temporary and untrained officers must be incorporated and the whole training system suffers. As in many aspects of instruction in modern society, the tasks of the teacher become more and more difficult to accomplish. The teachers must be more professionalized and more highly trained, and a lag in the upgrading of training personnel is often conspicuous in the military.

A suggestive study by Hanan Selvin demonstrates how leadership style influences the outcome of basic training, and indicates the potentials for creating a social climate appropriate for assimilating civilian recruits.[15] Using categories similar to the original Lewin-Lippitt-White group dynamics experiment, the investigator was able to identify three types of leadership at work in an infantry basic training installation which reflect the changes in military discipline. First, there was the arbitrary climate in which leadership operated by fear and with no admiration; second, there was the climate of the team concept—the persuasive climate—based on admiration for the leaders and without fear; and, finally, there was what was called a weak climate—the leaders were merely organizers and were neither arbitrary nor persuasive. Selvin found that positive identification with company leadership was most likely in the persuasive climate, much less in the weak climate, and least likely in the arbitrary climate. By investigating the leisure-time activities of the recruits, the researcher was able to observe how the arbitrary climate generated the highest levels of tension, so that the accumulated frustration of basic training had to be worked off in more violent, deviant, and extreme leisure-time activities.

Hand-in-hand with the shock treatment, older forms of training placed emphasis on mechanical and repetitive drill, plus an overwhelming concern with the personal appearance of the individual recruit. With the change in training techniques toward the team concept, there has also been an effort to introduce the recruit to realistic military problems. The military establishment did not abandon its tradition of "drill-type" training voluntarily and easily. In the ground force the refashioning of training toward realistic problem-solving came gradually and as a result of failures of the older techniques in battle in World War II. In naval and air units, training by its very nature is more realistic, since every training mission presents genuine hazards.

In problem-solving training the objective is to familiarize personnel with the environmental situations that they may have to face. Military personnel do not succeed merely by habit, but rather because of their intelligence and adaptability. Once the recruit has mastered basic techniques, his unit is given simulated problems of actual battle conditions. Dress parade is replaced by fire demonstration. Yet in the cold war, once the immediate pressure of combat requirements is removed, the tendency is to slip back into traditional forms. Much of military life becomes garrison life at the expense of realistic training, for "militarism" flourishes best in peacetime. In the context of garrison life, "spit and polish" has reemerged—often under the label of required discipline. As a result, the typical recruit—including many who have professional career ambitions—finds himself in a conflicted setting and unable to understand the relevance of his training experiences.

This tension is carefully documented in a study by Richard Christie of 48 squads involved in the basic infantry training cycle at Fort Dix during the summer of 1952.[16] One of the effects of basic training was an improvement in the recruit's personal adjustment—as measured by his perception of himself as being in good physical and psychological condition—and in positive relations with his peers. Thus, basic training did succeed in developing self-esteem and a sense of social solidarity among recruits. On the other hand, attitudes toward the institutional aspects of military life and of authority figures in the Army (officers and "noncoms") became more negative. In delineating the factors which assisted in adjustment to basic infantry training, the study revealed that recruits who remained in contact with their homes and family made the poorest adjustment to military training. Contact with home depended on whether the recruit's residence was close to the military base or at a greater distance. In short, the results give some support to aspects of the shock approach to training, so far as a clear separation from home is concerned. Furthermore, the structure of role relations in the squad could be modified to increase adjustment during basic training. Involvement of trainees in the leadership hierarchy on a rotation basis produced a strikingly more positive adjustment than those who had no such opportunity.

As the armed forces come to depend more and more upon professional volunteers, the tasks of training change, but there is no reason to believe that these tasks become more manageable. To the contrary, the resistance to "spit and polish" by the citizen-soldier and the reservist forces the military hierarchy to rethink its training procedures. A professional military establishment runs the risk of selecting personnel who will more readily conform, with the result that the assimilation process becomes routine and mechanical, rather than concerned with initiative and problem-solving. The dynamics of assimilation during the training phase is a problem in the military establishment that lends itself to sociological research; the available empirical data are still meagre.

Career Development

Since the skills and orientations which the new recruit—especially the officer candidate—is given during his initial assimilation are not necessarily appropriate for the later phases of his career, all services have developed extensive educational systems for retraining and for career development. Because combat is actually infrequent, the military establishment seems to expend much of its effort in training and retraining. In fact, the typical professional officer spends almost one-quarter of his career in school or in training situations. For the individual officer this can be a difficult and painful process; for the organization, it means facing the equally unpleasant fact that persons who were successful early in their careers may not show aptitudes for later career requirements and vice versa. One of the main functions of higher education in staff and command school and war college is to assist the officer in adjusting to the organizational patterns of higher echelons.

The organizational dilemmas linked to career development form a basic theme of military life. The dominant role conflict is the conflict between tactical combat skills and the requirements of higher command. Often this is stated as the clash between staff and command. But a close examination of the military establishment seems to indicate that the dilemma is between differing leadership skills. The skill of organizing and directly controlling small tactical units where the demonstration of technical skill is paramount gives way to the skill of organizing larger and more complex units where the elements of stress are more indirect and subtle. The military is no different from other institutions, in that the higher the position the less important specific technical skills are, and the more important are general interpersonal skills. A different and less important dilemma in the career of the officer, especially in the middle ranks, is the role conflict between operational commander and teacher. The outstanding officer is given many opportunities for teaching, and teaching is often an excellent technique for developing the skills required for higher administration. Successful teaching at the service academies is considered an important step toward higher command. However, the shift from tactical unit command to teaching produces deep and often frustrating tensions,[17] which interfere with an officer's performance.

The classical military solution to the dilemmas of career development has been to maintain the belief that the officer must be a generalist. Each of the services has developed a set of assumptions as to the components of an ideal military career and its educational system is geared to the development of this career line. Like all organization "myths," these assumptions are essentially correct in indicating the paths of advancement, but in many cases they can be inadequate in preparing personnel for emerging tasks. Officer education has developed from basic levels: officer candidate training—in the service academies and at civilian universities; tactical and technical training—at specialized service schools; junior command training—at the staff and command schools; and, finally, strategic training at the war colleges of the different services or at the national war college. A detailed description of the military educational system is presented by John W. Masland and Laurence I. Radway in a volume entitled *Soldiers and Scholars*.[18]

Military education has been subjected to the criticism that it has been isolated from the main intellectual currents. In particular, instruction in the basic disciplines (nonmilitary subjects) has suffered because the instructors have not been specialists. Military education has, in fact, been a form of self-education, and often the instruction has represented a service orientation rather than a fundamental educational experience. Nevertheless, since World War II military education has come under intense self-scrutiny, partly because it is clear that the highly trained technical specialist of atomic warfare can be trained for higher degrees in natural science and engineering only in civilian universities. Some effort to increase competence of officer-teachers in the social sciences has also taken place by sending them to leading universities. Of recent graduates from West Point 40 per cent are receiving graduate training at civilian centers. More civilians have been attached to the war college staffs. But since the objectives of a general military education remain rather vague, the curriculum of the military education system is in a state of flux. An interesting effort has been undertaken by a group of social scientists under Ralph W. Tyler to study the curriculum of the Air University, and to develop standards by which to guide its construction. The U.S. Military Academy, using its own resources, has launched a study of its graduates as an initial step in modifying its curriculum.

The most noteworthy result of the military education system has been, directly and indirectly, to reserve a preponderance of the highest military posts for the graduates of the military academies, as the following data attest.

The fact that approximately 40 per cent of those who reach the rank of general officer have not passed through the military academies is a result of the infusion of personnel into the military establishment during major wars. It is also due to the fact that those having specialized roles, such as physicians, must of necessity be trained outside the service academies. While in the nine-

GENERAL OFFICERS OF U.S. ARMY, NAVY, AIR FORCE, BY
TYPE OF MILITARY EDUCATION, 1951

| Rank | Total | Academy graduates | | | Non-academy Graduates |
		West Point	VMI[a]	Annapolis	
Army					
General of the Army	4	3	1	–	–
General	4	3	1	–	–
Lieutenant General	18	11	–	–	7
Major General	145	54	5	1	85
Brigadier General	199	116	1	1	81
Total	370	187	8	2	173
Navy					
Fleet Admiral	3	–	–	3	–
Admiral	5	–	–	5	–
Vice Admiral	21	–	–	21	–
Rear Admiral	220	–	–	177	43
Total	249	–	–	206	43
Air Force					
General	4	3	–	–	1
Lieutenant General	13	4	–	–	9
Major General	95	52	–	–	43
Brigadier General	135	69	–	–	66
Total	247	128	–	–	119

[a] An additional number were graduates of the selected list of private military academies and state universities which offer equivalent programs.

SOURCE: Official Army Register, Adjutant General's Office, 1951; Register of Commissioned Officers, Naval Personnel Bureau, 1951; and Air Force Register, Office of the Air Adjutant, 1951.

teenth century the role of the military academies was subject to constant public criticism, the recognized need for professionalized training in recent decades has resulted in a decline of this type of criticism. However, within the service, the issue is still alive as between academy and nonacademy graduates. The basic fact is that all of the armed forces are obliged to make use of cadres of junior and middle-level officers who are likely to have limited opportunities for advancement to the highest rank. As a result, this status difference generates organizational cleavages. There is every indication that in the future the percentage of nonacademy graduates in the officer corps will decline rather than increase. Thus, military education at all levels will have to continue to modify its content and procedures so as to guarantee adequate and fundamental preparation of higher officers.

Perhaps the most crucial question that sociological research can raise about the contemporary military educational system is whether it will produce future high-ranking military officers who will have a unified military establishment point of view rather than a more limited service point of view. Some light is thrown on this issue as the result of an investigation of a sample of higher officers (550) assigned to the Office of Secretary of Defense, to the Joint Staff, and to each of the three service headquarters. The investigation was an outgrowth of the Henry, Masland, and Radway inquiry of military education.[19] On the basis of written answers supplied by these officers in a questionnaire, the ambiguous character of present orientations toward unification is apparent. The authors conclude, "The study indicates that officers assigned to the Joint Staff and to the Office of Secretary of Defense share the 'broad non-service' values required in joint and national planning of defense policy." They add quickly that "supporting institutional arrangements are not believed to be wholly in keeping with the required values." This is the result of the frustrations that develop because the broadly oriented officers are uncertain that their careers will be advanced.

The data actually presented seem to underscore frustrations, rather than to demonstrate the presence of broad nonservice orientations, especially at the headquarters of the three services. Therefore, the question can still be investigated whether the present military educational system is sufficiently different from the past to ensure the development of an orientation that Secretary Lovett called the "broad nonservice" view.

NOTES TO CHAPTER III

[1] De Tocqueville, Alexis, *Democracy in America*, edited by Philip Bradley. Alfred A. Knopf, New York, 1946, vol. 2, chaps. 22 and 23.

Samuel Stouffer and others in *The American Soldier* report data on the pervasive extent to which social mobility and occupational training conditioned enlisted men's preference for branch of service, *op. cit.*, vol. 1, pp. 314–315.

See also Eli Ginzberg's *The Negro Potentials*, Columbia University Press, New York, 1956. This report concludes that the most spectacular increases in the opportunities of Negroes during the past generation have occurred in the armed forces.

[2] Kluckhohn, Clyde, *American Culture and Military Life*. January, 1951, mimeographed.

[3] Shils, Edward A., "The Contribution of the American Soldier to the Study of Primary Groups," in *Studies in the Scope and Method of "The American Soldier"*

edited by Robert Merton and Paul F. Lazarsfeld. The Free Press, Glencoe, Ill., 1950, pp. 35–36.

⁴ Stouffer, Samuel A., and others, *op. cit.*, vol. 1, pp. 122–124, 144–145.

⁵ Mattick, Hans W., *Parole to the Army:* A Research Report on Felons Paroled to the Army During World War II. Presented at the 87th Annual Congress of Corrections in Chicago, Ill., August, 1957.

⁶ Suchman, Edward A., Robin M. Williams, Jr., and Rose K. Goldsen, "Student Reaction to Impending Military Service," *American Sociological Review*, vol. 18, June, 1953, pp. 293–304.

⁷ Jenkins, William O., "A Review of Leadership Studies with Particular Reference to Military Problems," *Psychological Bulletin*, vol. 44, January, 1947, pp. 54–77.

⁸ Sanford, Fillmore H., "Research on Military Leadership" in *Current Trends:* Psychology in the World Emergency, Stephen Collins Foster Memorial Lectures, Dept. of Psychology, University of Pittsburgh, University of Pittsburgh Press, 1952, pp. 20–21. See also C. L. Shartle's "Studies in Naval Leadership: Part I" in *Groups, Leadership and Men*, edited by Harold S. Guetzkow, Carnegie Press, Pittsburgh, 1951, pp. 119–133, for a summary of the leadership studies conducted at Ohio State University.

⁹ This observation was first documented by research carried out during World War I by S. C. Kohs and K. W. Irle; see their "Prophesying Army Promotion," *Journal of Applied Psychology*, vol. 4, March, 1920, pp. 73–87. Literally dozens of studies have been repeated with little additional clarification of this complex issue.

¹⁰ Egbert, Robert L., and others; *Fighter I:* An Analysis of Combat Fighters and Non-Fighters. Technical Report no. 44, Human Resources Research Office, George Washington University, Washington, D. C., December, 1957, p. 68.

¹¹ Mandelbaum, David G., "Psychiatry in Military Society," *Human Organization*, vol. 13, Fall, 1954, pp. 5–15; Winter, 1955, pp. 19–25.

¹² Harris, Henry, *The Group Approach to Leadership-Testing*. Routledge and Kegan Paul, London, 1949.

¹³ U.S. Office of Strategic Services, Assessment Staff, *Assessment of Men*. Rinehart and Co., New York, 1948.

¹⁴ Goodacre, D. M., III, "The Use of a Sociometric Test as a Predictor of Combat Unit Effectiveness," *Sociometry*, vol. 14, May-August, 1951, pp. 148–153.

¹⁵ Selvin, Hanan Charles, *The Effects of Leadership Climate on the Non-Duty Behavior of Army Trainees*. Unpublished doctoral dissertation, Columbia University, New York, 1956.

¹⁶ Christie, Richard, *An Experimental Study of Modification in Factors Influencing Recruits' Adjustment to the Army*. Research Center for Human Relations, New York University, 1953, mimeographed.

¹⁷ Getzels, J. W., and E. C. Guba, "Role and Role Conflict and Effectiveness: An Empirical Study," *American Sociological Review*, vol. 19, April, 1954, pp. 164–175. The teaching staffs at the Air University were the subject of this research.

¹⁸ Masland, John W., and Laurence I. Radway, *Soldiers and Scholars*. Princeton University Press, Princeton, N. J., 1957.

¹⁹ Henry, Andrew F., John W. Masland, and Laurence I. Radway, "Armed Forces Unification and the Pentagon Officer," *Public Administration Review*, vol. 15, Summer, 1955, pp. 173–180.

PRIMARY GROUPS AND
MILITARY EFFECTIVENESS

THE ASPECT OF MILITARY ORGANIZATION that has received the most attention from social scientists has been the role of primary groups in maintaining organizational effectiveness. By primary groups sociologists mean those small social groupings in which social behavior is governed by intimate face-to-face relations. During World War II many sociologists in the armed forces were impressed with the crucial contribution of cohesive primary group relations to morale, especially in situations of stress. Many of them discovered that, before their personal experience in military service, they had overemphasized the importance of ideological and political values in conditioning the effectiveness of military formations. Their experiences in the armed forces led them to discover or to rediscover primary groups in other complex organizations, such as the educational system, the factory, and the government agency.

The crucial role of satisfactory man-to-man relations in combat effectiveness was a universal observation during World War II. The psychiatrists Roy R. Grinker and John P. Speigel summarized their work in the Air Force with this statement: "The men seem to be fighting more for someone than against somebody." Analysis of group cohesion of the Wehrmacht produced these two hypotheses among others:

> 1. It appears that a soldier's ability to resist is a function of the capacity of his immediate primary group (his squad or section) to avoid social disintegration. When the individual's immediate group, and its supporting formations, met his basic organic needs, offered him affection and esteem from both officers and comrades, supplied

him with a sense of power and adequately regulated his relations with authority, the element of self-concern in battle, which would lead to disruption of the effective functioning of his primary group, was minimized.

2. The capacity of the primary group to resist disintegration was dependent on the acceptance of political, ideological, and cultural symbols (all secondary symbols) only to the extent that these secondary symbols became directly associated with primary gratifications. . . .[1]

The trained combat observer and military historian S. L. A. Marshall states the same conclusion: "I hold it to be one of the simplest truths of war that the thing which enables an infantry soldier to keep going with his weapons is the near presence or the presumed presence of a comrade."

Yet it is necessary to bear in mind that cohesive primary groups do not just occur but are fashioned and developed by complex military institutions. At most, primary groups operate to impose standards of behavior—in garrison life and in combat—and to interpret the demands of military authority for the individual soldier. The goals and standards that primary groups enforce are hardly self-generated; they arise from the larger military environment and from the surrounding civilian society.

In the empirical study of primary groups, it is not sufficient to investigate the factors that make for cohesive social relations in the smallest tactical units. This can be highly misleading, since primary groups can be highly cohesive and yet impede the goals of military organization.[2] Cohesive primary groups contribute to organizational effectiveness when the standards of behavior they enforce are articulated with the requirements of formal authority. This was not the case in segregated Negro units where primary group norms led the men to feel that their personal dignity was being depreciated by military authority.

Social Cohesion

Social cohesion in primary groups, military or other, is affected both by the social backgrounds of group members and the immediate social situation. In the military establishment common social background assists the members in developing intimate interpersonal relations; similarities in social experience supply a meaningful basis for responding to military life. From a personality standpoint, the ability to offer and to receive affection in an all-male society forms the basis of primary group solidarity. The social isolate is not a military asset and is likely to weaken social cohesion. A variety of studies, including *The American Soldier*, psychiatric observations, and the studies mentioned on social solidarity during training, seem to indicate that to some degree family stability, especially satisfactory identification with one's father, contributes to the ability to participate in primary groups. But this is only a partial statement, since it does not rule out the fact that strong emotions and even strong neurotic impulses may help a person mobilize himself to meet a military crisis. The capacity of personality to enter into intimate group relations in groups under stress is not well understood.

Moreover, it is not necessary to assume that cohesion in primary groups can only be the result of uniformity or like-mindedness among its members. To the contrary, a division of labor and a blending of perspectives can be the basis of group cohesion. What is crucial from the point of view of the military establishment is that the members of the smallest tactical units have gone through some trying group experiences which demonstrate to them the value of social solidarity.

Thus, along with social and psychological background factors, social cohesion of primary groups in the military derives from the organizational realities under which military personnel must operate. For example, this would include for each man: the technical aspects of his weapons, the type of organization of his unit and its replacement system, the nature of the military threat he has to face, and the performance of his immediate leaders.

First, the technical dimensions of the weapons systems impose limitations on stability and cohesiveness in military primary groups. Is the weapon fired as a team or is it fired by an individual? The increased importance of the primary group concept is an outgrowth of the trend in weapons which requires that more and more personnel operate technically as teams. Even the individual fighter has been outmoded in the infantry where the rifleman is trained to be a member of a team.

Nevertheless, there is wide variation in the amount of communication and in the difficulty of communication between a closely knit submarine crew and a widely dispersed infantry unit. In some weapons systems it has been possible to develop a social definition of a tour of duty: 30 to 50 missions of a bomber crew. On the other hand, for the tank crew—in part, because of irregular commitment to combat—such a definition is impossible. Some weapons systems involve the aggressive expenditure of energy against a visible enemy, for example, the fighter pilot engaged in strafing. Others require only a mechanical routine against a distant target—for example, heavy artillery units. The amount of support a person receives from his primary group varies accordingly.

While generalizations in this area are most hazardous, it does seem that weapons systems which maintain close physical proximity of team members and enhance the process of communication contribute most to primary group cohesion. Moreover, weapons systems are accorded differential prestige in the military establishment, and the higher the prestige of the weapon the greater the contribution to group solidarity. The weapon becomes part of the self-image of the person, and the more powerful the weapon, the greater its contribution to the battle, and the greater is the person's sense of potency and group solidarity. Social cohesion in primary groups is not merely a human phenomenon; it is an outgrowth of environmental conditions, and in the military this means the technical dimensions of the various weapons systems.

Second, the type of unit organization, including the personnel replacement system of the U.S. military establishment, has certain consequences for group cohesion that are worthy of study. To the foreign observer, the American military establishment—and this includes all services—appears to be a "mass-produced" institution in which little effort is made to build on previous loyalties or to maintain organizational continuity. The replacement system stands at variance with many European military formations, which have in the past sought to draw their men from similar geographical locales or to maintain the identity of military formations. In the United States it is as if a democracy felt that randomization of assignment would ensure better distribution of risks and the destruction of units with military traditions would guarantee civilian supremacy. To some degree, this has been American policy.

Since World War I, in which units from specific geographical localities suffered disproportionately, ground force policy has tended to avoid geographical assignment. The competition of the services with the state-organized reserve system has also tended in this direction. Absence of a desire for the preservation of traditional units within which to develop a stable and cohesive primary group structure is a reflection of the lack of concern with traditions in American society. But beyond this, it represents a technological orientation to problems of organizational effectiveness. While new machines are likely to be better than old ones, constantly disrupted organizations are not necessarily more conducive to satisfactory primary group relations.

One can argue that technical requirements of warfare have made geographically recruited units impossible and have rendered the preservation of traditional units most difficult. Nevertheless, the mass-produced character of the American military establishment is exaggerated in its replacement system, which tends to treat replacements as individual components rather than as group members.

When men do not know each other, combat units suffer in effectiveness. The loss of a single member can be most disruptive to an air crew; the new replacement must develop a sense of solidarity with his team. This is particularly the case in airborne units, with their high attrition rate. In a study of some 70 tactical episodes of operation Neptune, the airborne phase of the Normandy invasion, it was found that only a minor fraction was successful if the original unit was disrupted during the drop. If an officer or a noncommissioned officer collected a group of men he had never commanded and tried to lead them into battle, the results were almost uniformly unsatisfactory. The same observations were made from a study of battle stragglers in the Ardennes operation; individual stragglers had little combat value when put into a strange organization.

Since weapons require teams of men rather than individuals, modification of organization, replacement, and assignment practices have become essential. Yet military management has tended to lag behind technological realities. The ground forces have only slowly modified their standard operating procedures which handle transfers and replacements on an individual person basis. In World War II and in Korea the individual soldier often had to be detached and removed from his training squad and sent to a line squad already in combat, where he had not had previous personal contacts. This practice was extensive during the period of the prolonged truce negotiations in Korea when individual replacements were required to implement the rotation system then in effect. Ground force regulations have been revised to permit four "buddies" rather than individuals to be transferred. Although this is relevant for social cohesion, military effectiveness depends on the maintenance of continuity in larger units.[3]

In the contemporary military establishment the greatest concern for organizational stability can be found in those units that are maintained in a constant state of alert for immediate commitment. In these units, replacements are more often handled as units, and there is greater emphasis on the movement of whole tactical formations as units. Increased mobility can make it possible to move whole units out of and back to home bases. The system of alert in the Strategic Air Command where each crew has a permanent continental base, is an example of a case in point.

In the cold war establishment the maintenance of conditions required for primary group solidarity is yet to be achieved. Many units operate at less than full strength with a constant turnover of personnel. In all three services the return to civilian employment is considerable, especially at the junior officer level. In the air and naval units, the short-term reservist presents special problems in maintaining social cohesion. In the ground force, where the two-year service for selectees operates, there is a constant rotation of personnel after basic training. The observations of a young sociologist in the military service between 1954 and 1955 are most revealing.

> Soon after basic training, the company is split up and groups of individuals are sent to separate stations. Even when a group from the basic training unit is sent to the same permanent station, before their army career is over, it is highly probable that there will occur further transfers among them, thus atomizing the group which may have common memories and a certain amount of solidarity. The draftee sees other individuals being transferred from unit to unit. There develops an expectation that shifting station is a routine occurrence in the army. The draftee prepared himself for this by not involving himself more than necessary with any group to which he happens to be transferred. Any great psychological involvement with a single primary group, when a shift is possible at any moment, is very frustrating.[4]

Third, social cohesion in primary groups is influenced by the proximity of danger and the importance of the mission which the group is assigned. Up to a point, as the threat of the danger increases and as the importance of the mission becomes apparent, the social cohesion of primary groups increases. This is the great difference between peacetime and wartime military establishments; this is the difference between garrison life and realistic training exercises, or between port duty and life with the fleet "in being." But what is the nature of the perceived threat in the cold war establishment, and how does a sense of mission influence social cohesion under conditions that require maintaining a state of alert, rather than responding to an actual military threat?

For the great bulk of the military establishment, organizational life is an 8 to 4:30 job, with interruption for field training or administrative emergencies. Residence off the military establishment, the proximity of family, and the importance of civilian contacts dilute the sense of urgent military mission. In units on the alert, the function of the primary group is not only to prepare the individual for the pressures of combat but also to train him to withstand the tensions of maintaining a state of operational readiness. Training becomes an end in itself and those who perform well must receive special benefits.

Fourth, social cohesion in combat or in cold war depends on the performance of small unit leaders. For the contemporary military establishment with its emphasis on group consensus, tactical leadership must be based on example and demonstrated competence. As late as World War I, British officers carried the swagger stick as a ritualistic symbol of their command. Since their authority was based on social position and on direct domination, they had to demonstrate that they were different from the men whom they commanded. They would not carry weapons. They carried only a stick, yet they were able to get their men to fight. Today leaders must continuously demonstrate their fighting and technical ability in order that they may command without resort to arbitrary and ultimate sanctions. George Homans' analysis of "The Small Warship" illustrates how naval authority, despite its traditional basis, is also grounded in technical competence.[5] The military leader is a member of a team even after he has risen from tactical command. He must continue to demonstrate his fighter spirit; witness the Air Force generals who insist on flying their own planes, and the United Nations commander in Korea who carried two hand grenades.

Combined with leadership by example, the military leader is required to display his interest and affection for his men. He must be interested in their physical and psychological well-being. He must share their discomforts in order not to weaken social cohesion with them. Such concerns border on intimacy, and traditional-minded officers are often fearful that social intimacy may involve an undermining of authority. In fact, social intimacy in the cold war establishment does run the risk of developing personal cliques which disrupt solidarity.[6] With the breakdown of the older forms of domination, and the emergence of indirect controls, the degree of social intimacy between officers and enlisted men, and among enlisted men, becomes an area of ambiguity and stress. But when the fear of intimacy creates a barrier to social cohesion, morale becomes mechanical and military formations lose their vitality.

These conflicts arise because tactical leaders must regulate the relations of their unit with higher authority. The commander is required by his men to defend them against arbitrary and unwarranted intrusion from above. Yet the officer in the tactical unit is also the final representative of coercive higher authority. For him to overidentify with his men would impair the system of authority. In the U.S. military establishment it is typically the senior noncommissioned officer on whom this role conflict devolves, and who has the task of adjudicating conflicting pressures. A suggestive study of the first sergeant in the Air Force highlights this process.[7] Squadron officers, it was found, tend to favor less authority or responsibility for first sergeants, while the first sergeants themselves and their subordinates favor more authority. In turn, the first sergeants would like to spend more time attending to the personal needs of airmen, and doing less paper work. By inference, junior officers would like to enhance their authority, but they are not prepared or permitted to display the direct contact with enlisted men that such increased authority would require.

A special problem in social cohesion has been the integration of Negro troops into primary group structures. Primary group structures can become incompatible with the requirements of military organization when the criterion for making the assignment is a group characteristic such as race or ethnic origin. Grounded in social prejudices and justified on the basis that unsegregated units could not develop intimate and stable man-to-man relations, military manpower policies have in the past prevented Negro personnel from being used effectively.

The process of desegregation in the armed forces has been a dramatic achievement in military management. It has also been a powerful verification of sociological theory concerning social cohesion and organizational effectiveness. Sociological theory does not hold that segregated units would under all conditions weaken organizational effectiveness. The experience of the Japanese-American battalions attest to the contrary. This is a case where segregation did not prevent Japanese-Americans from achieving group goals, namely, demonstrating their loyalty and articulating effectively with the authority structure. Segregation of Negro troops worked to opposite ends. The outcome was to prevent the development of groups with social cohesion committed to the military hierarchy.

The first evidence of the feasibility of eliminating segregation emerged when the Navy initiated its program of utilization of Negroes in combat assignments. Some research evidence was collected from a number of infantry companies which, in the closing phases of the campaign in Northwest Europe, had Negro platoons attached.[8] In the Korean conflict, battle conditions required the final breakdown of segregation, which was being pressed with greater vigor by civilian political leaders. The details of sociological research into the process of desegregation in Korea have not been made available for scientific publication. But the assumption of inherent differential capacities of Negroes for combat has been clearly laid to rest for all except the fanatically prejudiced. One of the implications, which will be crucial should civilian society press for residential desegregation, is that the process is made feasible if a limitation is imposed on the concentration of Negroes assigned to a given area or unit.

Group Behavior Under Stress

At some point continued exposure of any military group to stress begins to produce a weakening of primary group solidarity, and an undermining of organizational effectiveness. One of the direct manifestations of disintegration, which can easily be observed and charted, is the nature and rate of psychoneurotic breakdowns. Every soldier will manifest behavior of a neurotic or psychotic variety if subject to severe stress long enough.

On the basis of studies in North Africa and Italy during World War II, a time limit was estimated beyond which the American combat infantry soldier could not be expected to resist psychiatric breakdown. After prolonged exposure to combat, the infantryman "wore out, either developing an acute incapacitating neurosis or else becoming hypersensitive to shell fire, so overly cautious and jittery that he was ineffective and demoralizing to the newer men."[9] The point at which this occurred appears to have come somewhere between 200 and 400 aggregate days of combat. Peak effectiveness seems to have been reached between three months and five months of combat.

This is an estimate for one combat situation. The British command estimated twice as long a period, since it was British policy to afford more brief intervals of relief from frontline duty than was American practice. The nature of the battle also affects the process of breakdown. In general, the rate of psychoneurotic casualties rises in proportion to the rate of those wounded and killed. An important exception occurs during full retreat. Under full retreat psychiatric casualties may not be able to save themselves, but it does appear that in such situations the danger to the whole group overrides the inclination of individual soldiers to manifest psychoneurotic behavior. In periods of rapid advance, the rate also drops off sharply.

The psychiatric rate also varied among branches of service and among different armed forces, as a careful review of research evidence on social environmental factors in military psychiatry by David G. Mandelbaum demonstrates.[10] There are very few psychiatric cases among U.S. submarine crews. To be sure, submarine crews are carefully selected, but since the stress of this service is extreme, social organizational factors, namely, the intimate organization of submarine life, must be operative.[11] A similar pattern held true for bomber crews in World War II, who developed tightly knit primary groups. In the Bomber Command of the RAF, for example, the casualty rate during World War II was reported at 64 per cent, including those who were killed, wounded, missing, and injured. Nevertheless, the psychiatric breakdown rate was only about 5 per cent.

Differences in cultural background and "national character" seem to influence the rate and type of psychiatric breakdown in combat. When newly captured German prisoners of war and their British captors in North Africa were both subjected to air attack, it has been reported that the Germans displayed much less neurotic behavior. Similarly Indian units fighting in the Arakan jungles showed a lower incidence of neurotic behavior than British units in the same area. The Yugoslav partisans had a high incidence of hysterical convulsions, a symptom not at all common in the American army. In the Japanese army hysteria was also the most common reaction to prolonged stress. Many observers have noted that the incidence of psychoneurotic breakdown among American soldiers was not only a reaction to the fear of being killed; often anxiety or guilt that was created over the fear of killing someone acted as the precipitating factor. Clearly, fundamental social taboos of civilian life were at work here.

Psychiatric breakdown can also be delayed as a result of social factors. The most dramatic case was the low rate of neurotic behavior of the German civilian population under air attack, a rate which remained low until 1948 when deep-seated psychiatric symptoms began to appear as living conditions improved. The same delayed pattern was present among German prisoners of war, who had a lower rate than combat soldiers, but whose symptoms emerged after release from captivity. Thus, it has been documented by research too extensive to survey that reactions to combat stress—as reflected by the incidence of psychiatric casualties—are influenced not only by the military situation but by social environmental and group factors as well.

During World War II and the Korean conflict military psychiatrists became aware of social environmental aspects of psychoneurotic breakdowns, and treatment procedures were modified in order to render effective support. Civilian psychiatry had its limitations in military settings and the recent history of military psychiatry is a dramatic example of practical sociology developed on the spot.

At the beginning of World War II the American medical services followed the practice of rapidly evacuating psychiatric casualties to rear hospitals. The result was that there were very few who resumed combat duty. Treatment was designed to deal with manifested symptoms by assisting the discharge of anxiety. The therapist, under these situations, tended to identify with the needs of the patient, and was impelled to promise relief from future combat duty. The psychiatrist was operating as a "remote spectator of the battle rather than a forward observer." Military psychiatry became effective by changing its organizational setting. By installing forward psychiatric-clearing stations, and by handling psychiatric casualties in the combat zone, the approach of the psychiatrists changed. They recognized that combat brought forth group identifications which sustained soldiers. Psychiatrists were able to make use of these group identifications—the desire of the soldier not to abandon his buddies—and, as a result, the rate returned to combat increased.

The rate of psychiatric breakdown is but one index of military group behavior under stress. It is one that has dominated thinking about primary groups under stress because of the abundance of impressionistic observations and the dramatic quality of psychiatric symptoms. But alternative frames of reference are necessary to encompass the dynamics of primary groups under extreme conditions. Thus, Bruno Bettelheim, on the basis of his participant observation of human behavior in the extreme situation of the Nazi concentration camp, brought to attention the process of identification with the aggressor—the process by which some inmates, in order to preserve a human identity, abandoned their own identity and assumed that of the guards who were persecuting them.[12]

Under stress of combat, as soon as a military formation encounters enemy resistance, long before psychiatric breakdown occurs, there is a tendency for communications between group members to decrease and to break down temporarily. The task of the unit commander is to reestablish these communication networks. The fighter pilot on his first real mission feels completely isolated and his behavior may threaten his own formation. In the infantry, where group members are not physically held together as a submarine crew is, the group literally falls apart under the impact of enemy firepower. Panic almost never occurs. The failure of a high proportion of infantry soldiers to use their weapons in combat is partly due to this breakdown of communications. The reluctance of the soldier to fire under these circumstances is not that by firing he will expose himself to additional danger. That is much too rational a consideration. He is under shock, confronted by a strange situation in which he feels completely on his own. Only when the combat group learns to behave as a team do its members become militarily useful. Realistic training, aggressive leadership, and mere survival through the initial onslaught, all of these help to overcome the disruptions of stress.

The experiences in Korea corroborate the studies of World War II on the linkages of primary groups in combat with the larger military and social environment. For the enlisted men, and even for many officers, their perspectives were limited to their immediate tactical unit—the company and the squadron. Under the stress of battle, whenever there is a weakening of communications, the feeling develops that higher authority is acting capriciously and arbitrarily. The layers of military authority were remote and distant except for those few officers who had sustained contact with higher command. Civilian society penetrated into the daily life of combat personnel only by means of family contacts. Secondary symbols of ideology, even those of race and religion, were indeed faint while political concern was almost nonexistent.

Only one detailed participant observational study of the dynamics of primary groups was prepared for the Korean conflict. This dealt with an infantry company from November, 1952, through February, 1953, during the period of stalemate and was prepared by Captain Roger William Little.[13] This was the period in which the mainline of resistance had become stabilized in bunkers and trenchlike emplacements, and hostilities were limited to patrols, sporadic raids, and artillery duels, which could be fierce and destructive of personnel. The rotation system continually disrupted personnel attachments, to the point of causing concern among commanders about military effectiveness. Under these circumstances it was understandable that masculine norms and the need to establish one's manliness played much less a role than in the aggressive and attack phase of the conflict.

Roger Little's investigation highlights that under these special tactical conditions a much more primitive type of primary group solidarity developed than in World War II. The essential and basic unit of social cohesion was a two-man relationship rather than a squad social grouping. The squad was too dispersed and its personnel rotated too rapidly to develop effective cohesion.

The "buddy" relation was a cohesive unit built around risk; it was the person a soldier felt he could rely on in case of danger. These relations were private knowledge; "one man could think of another buddy, but could never state it or boast of the attachments publicly." This attachment was a defense against isolation, and permitted the exchange of the most intimate communications and fears between two partners.

At some point, just as individuals become prone to psychiatric breakdown, one can observe that combat units under stress begin to show signs of social disintegration if replacements and relief are not adequate. For many weapons systems, the unit is forced because of mechanical reasons to carry on their military duties; there is no other way out. But a pattern of military disintegration has been identified by sociologists which reflects the disruption of primary group life as a result of the breakdown of communications, loss of leadership, or prolonged breaks in the supply of food and medicine. The individual soldier becomes concerned with his survival at the expense of his military assignment. *Last ditch resistance*, which ends only with the exhaustion of fighting equipment and subsequent surrender or death, implies the absence of social disintegration. As disintegration sets in, resistance becomes *routine;* that is, orders are followed but resistance is discontinued when the enemy becomes overwhelmingly powerful and aggressive. Further disintegration under stress can lead to *passive surrender*, that is, token resistance by allowing capture after nominal face-saving gestures or by mere nonresistance.

Extreme forms of disintegration often underlie *active surrender*, the deliberate decision to give up to the enemy or to take steps to facilitate capture. Finally, *desertion* is an outgrowth of the most active form of social disintegration, since it usually involves the individual soldier breaking with his primary group and deliberately going over to the enemy lines. While, as Dr. Henry Dicks has demonstrated, the deserter may frequently be a person with marked neurotic symptoms, this continuum of organizational disintegration of military units is not necessarily related to the increased state of psychiatric malaise.[14] It is more a group response to stress in which the fate of the group rather than the fate of the individual is paramount. This motivation operates among defectors from totalitarian nations during periods of cold war.

In military operations against totalitarian powers, the maintenance of group cohesion even after combat is of crucial importance. As well as resistance to indoctrination after capture, escape, evasion, and survival emerge as serious problems when theaters of war spread over vast distances and uninhabitable territories. The political objectives of Communist powers require them to treat prisoners as potential recruits.

In Korea, American prisoners of war were subjected to extensive pressure to collaborate with the enemy. Shock to the pride of the American public was immense when it learned that fellow Americans had turned traitor in Chinese prisoner-of-war camps. The belief developed that the Chinese Communist had perfected revolutionary techniques of indoctrination, but more careful and more detached estimates indicate that the techniques used were well known but had been applied with great intensity, although not always with great expertness or forethought.

The variation in response to Communist pressure and indoctrination was extreme. The early captured ground force personnel who seemed to come from units that had not developed high social cohesion and who suffered extensive mistreatment after capture apparently supplied the bulk of the collaborators. The events of the Korean conflict would indicate that the troops were not trained or prepared for the type of prisoner of war situation to which they were exposed. The defects in training were those that would have rendered them better soldiers, but it is problematic whether their resistance to Communist indoctrination would have been markedly different. Resistance in part was based on being a member of a military body and, therefore, the more effective the military body, the greater the potential for resistance.

This is underlined by the results of two carefully documented studies of the returned prisoners of war, which both conclude that there was a lack of correspondence between the extent to which prisoners were favorably impressed by the ideological doctrines of their captors and the degree to which they would go along with their captors in active collaboration.[15] Likewise, it is crucial to note that one of these studies by Albert Biderman on Air Force prisoners concludes that American characteristic tendencies, including a distrust of political dogma in general, and an aversion to Communist dogma, in particular, formed a basis of their resistance to Communist indoctrination. While efforts to interview the prisoners for psychiatric and legal purposes have resulted in the accumulation of a considerable amount of evidence on how individual soldiers behaved under stress of Communist indoctrination, the dynamics of the social organization of the Communist prison war camps have not been fully reported. Such an analysis might well reveal some of the sharp differences between various totalitarian practices. Because of the strategical background of the Korean conflict, U.S. efforts to maintain contact and support for the captured military personnel were markedly limited as compared with World War II; these dimensions would also have to be covered for a full understanding of American behavior under stress.

The dynamics of primary groups under military pressure are based on exposure to battle conditions involving high explosives. The Korean conflict, while not the last military conflict conducted with conventional weapons, represents a turning point. The character of social cohesion in the Korean battle, while essentially similar to that in World War II, had undergone modification. At the end the tremendous expenditure of firepower, and the resulting need for greater dispersion, seemed to produce a more primitive and more attenuated form of social solidarity. The growth of firepower had further segmented social relations.

Yet what relevance will the primary group concept have in years to come? Extrapolation from present trends may leave crucial questions unanswered. Future limited warfare will certainly involve units operating on the same principles of social cohesion as we know them now. Even in irregular warfare, which is the most frequent form of contemporary warfare, the same concepts seem readily applicable. But what about unlimited warfare, not in its unthinkable actuality, but in the prolonged preparation for deterring unlimited warfare? First, many combat units acting as agents of deterrence are not trained for prolonged combat but for single missions, implicitly one-way missions. What are the dynamics of social cohesion in such formations? The tension resulting from being continuously on the alert can be deeply devastating. Second, many military units will be required to have both a limited warfare and an unlimited warfare mission. Is this technically and organizationally feasible, and what does this mean for social solidarity and primary group cohesion? It is best for social scientists to assume that old concepts and theories still apply and then to be prepared to discover what is new. Much thought will have to be given to the problem of social cohesion in units using new types of weapons, such as submarines designed to remain underseas for prolonged periods, or highly mobile infantry units equipped with low-yield atomic tactical weapons, or the like. While the current interest in the human problems of new weapons is mainly physiological, it will ultimately be necessary to discover and rediscover the social elements in these weapons systems.

NOTES TO *CHAPTER IV*

[1] Shils, Edward A., and Morris Janowitz, "Cohesion and Disintegration in the Wehrmacht in World War II," *Public Opinion Quarterly*, vol. 12, Summer, 1948, pp. 280–315. See also Knut, Pipping, *Kompaniet Som Samhälle:* Iakttagelser I Ett Finskt Fontförband, 1941–1944, Abo Akademi, Abo, 1947 (The Social Life of a Machine Gun Company); contains English summary.

[2] A number of studies have been made of the dynamics of primary group relations in the armed forces without employing explicit criteria concerning the type of military behavior that primary group relations were supposed to produce. A typical example is R. L. Hall's "Social Influence on the Aircraft Commander's Role," *American Sociological Review*, vol. 20, June, 1955, pp. 292–299. These studies do not clarify the problems of organizational effectiveness.

[3] Chesler, David J., Niel J. Van Steenberg, and Joyce E. Brueckel, "Effect on Morale of Infantry Team Replacement and Individual Replacement Systems," *Sociometry*, vol. 18, December, 1955, pp. 587–597.

[4] Uyeki, Eugene S., "Sociology of the Cold War Army." Paper delivered at the American Sociological Society Convention, Seattle, Wash., 1958.

[5] Homans, George C., "The Small Warship," *American Sociological Review*, vol. 11, June, 1946, pp. 294–300.

[6] Simpson, Richard L., *Friendship Cliques in United States Air Force Wings.* Technical Report no. 3, Air Force Base Project, Institute for Research in Social Science, University of North Carolina, Chapel Hill, undated.

[7] Karcher, E. Kenneth, Jr., *The First Sergeant in the United States Air Force*. Technical Report no. 7, Air Force Base Project, Institute for Research in Social Science, University of North Carolina, Chapel Hill, October, 1952.

[8] Information and Education Division, Army Service Forces, U.S. War Department, Report no. B-157, 1945. Reprinted in *Readings in Social Psychology*, edited by Theodore M. Newcomb and Eugene Hartley, Henry Holt and Co., New York, 1947, pp. 542–546. See David G. Mandelbaum's *Soldier Groups and Negro Soldiers*, University of California Press, Berkeley, Calif., 1952, for an interpretive analysis of the problem.

[9] Appel, John W., and Gilbert W. Bebe, "Preventive Psychiatry," *Journal of the American Medical Association*, 1946, vol. 131, p. 1470.

[10] Mandelbaum, David G., "Psychiatry in Military Society," *Human Organization*, vol. 13, Fall, 1954, pp. 5–15; Winter, 1955, pp. 19–25.

[11] National Research Council Committee on Undersea Warfare, *A Survey Report on Human Factors in Undersea Warfare*, Washington, D. C., 1949, p. 29. See especially chapter by Ernest A. Haggard, "Psychological Causes and Results of Stress," pp. 441–461.

[12] Bettelheim, Bruno, "Individual and Mass Behavior in Extreme Situations," *Journal of Abnormal and Social Psychology*, vol. 36, October, 1943, pp. 417–452.

[13] Little, Roger William, *A Study of the Relationship Between Collective Solidarity and Combat Role Performance*. Unpublished doctoral dissertation, Michigan State University, East Lansing, Mich., 1955.

[14] These categories of group disintegration can be compared with the categories of individual reaction used in the Human Resources Research Office study of nonfighters in Korea: (1) actively withdrawn or "drug out," (2) withdrawn psychologically, (3) malingerers, (4) defensively overreacts, (5) becomes hysterically incapacitated. See Egbert, Robert L., and others, *Fighter I:* An Analysis of Combat Fighters and Non-Fighters, Technical Report no. 44, Human Resources Research Office, George Washington University, Washington, D. C., December, 1957, p. 14.

[15] Biderman, Albert D., *Effects of Communist Indoctrination Attempts:* Some Comments Based on an Air Force Prisoners of War Study, Document no. 134247, Air Force Personnel and Training Research Center, Lackland Air Force Base, Texas, Sept., 1947; Segal, J., *Factors Related to the Collaboration and Resistance Behavior of U.S. Army PW's in Korea*, Technical Report no. 33, Human Resources Research Office, George Washington University, Washington, D. C., December, 1956. The lack of unification in the armed forces pervades social science research as can be seen by the fact that both the Army and the Air Force studied their returned prisoners of war independently, but research on this point did produce independent validation. See also special issue of *Journal of Social Issues*, vol. 13, no. 3, 1957, on "Brainwashing."

V

TECHNIQUES OF ORGANIZATIONAL CONTROL

THE STYLE OF MILITARY ADMINISTRATION is to create a set of formal regulations and written directives which establish policy for all sorts of eventualities. The greater the imponderables and uncertainties that military command has to face, the more emphasis is placed on explicit orders, elaborate directives, and contingency plans.

First, military command structure is laid out and continually redesigned so as to create a precise format in which each unit is clearly charted and its tasks assigned. Organizational doctrine, although it varies from military service to military service, has its traditional objectives: direct lines of formal authority, explicit definition of missions, clear channels of official communication between staff and operating units, and limitations on the span of control.

Second, military command seeks to routinize its operating procedures to the most minute detail. The content of every sanction and reward is an official act. When General Eisenhower, during World War II, confirmed the death sentence for an infantry deserter to be carried out by a firing squad made up of members of his own regiment, the organizational manual was the sole source of guidance, inasmuch as this was the only case of its kind during World War II and the first since the Civil War. The manual supplied the mass of essential details from the mode of selecting the members of the firing squad to the issuance of the traditional blank cartridge. In the same vein, the Air Force manual on staff procedures is a multi-volumed compendium with never-ending supplements. This concern for reducing operating procedures to written directives creates the image of the military establishment as the most complete bureaucracy. The operating manuals of the American Telephone and Telegraph Company are no less detailed, but they do not encompass the vast range of topics that life in the military community entails.

Yet it is obvious that organizational charts and rule books do not describe the way in which large-scale organizations operate. Informal practices and personal communication networks are required if coordination is to be accomplished. The military establishment is no exception. Much of the sociological literature on organizational control is taken up with the influence of informal organization. Often the assumption is made, although it remains to be adequately documented, that the gap between formal organization and informal realities is greater in the military than in other complex bureaucracies. There are too few systematic empirical studies of organizational control to permit generalization about the interaction between formal authority and informal communications in the military.[1] Nevertheless, dilemmas of communication in military systems have been so often observed by social scientists that general mechanisms can be identified.

Communications and Command Channels

Sociologists agree that command channels and communication processes in the military establishment are not merely structural devices. Organizational control depends as much on what is communicated as on how it is communicated. Practitioners of administration and business management often tend to be concerned with "opening channels" of communication, regardless of policy content. Command channels and communications are effective or ineffective as a result of the policies that are transmitted. It is the system of rewards and sanctions that has been created to develop socially cohesive units and to weld them into an effective military system that will determine the outcome. No amount of communication will overcome extreme differentials between enlisted men and officers, nor will the best techniques of communications counterbalance lack of technical competence.

Command channels and communication processes in the military have their distinctive features. Like any large-scale organization, military command produces a downward flow of official and authoritative messages and instructions from the top to the bottom level. Yet informal messages flowing down from higher levels abound in the form of personal grapevines and deliberate informal prior notification of important decisions. One of the distinctive qualities of the military command channels is that these informal communications are required, since official communications tend to lag timewise behind organizational needs. These informal communications make it possible for personnel to prepare themselves and their units for new assignments and new tasks.

While informal downward channels are important to overcome time lags in official communications and command, the informal upward flow is even more crucial for effective organizational control. Military command has official procedures for maintaining an upward flow of information by means of reporting systems, technical chains of command, and official inspections. Nevertheless, the official flow of upward communication is less adequate than in other types of bureaucracies. The military must rely on elaborate forms of informal communications to keep higher echelons informed. In part, this is due to the vast size of the military establishment and, in part, to the speed with which organizational developments are effected. The informal and unofficial channels of communication are so important that they become institutionalized in the oral "briefing." At the highest levels of the Pentagon, one is struck by the heavy reliance on oral briefings, despite the military's concern with authoritative communications. The oral briefing is a rapid and flexible device for upward communications, which permits a more or less informal exchange of information. Since briefings are attended by many officials, they serve to bypass any single person who might bottleneck the upward flow of information.

All organizations have hierarchical systems which impede the upward flow of communications and force reliance on informal communications. It is possible that the military organization requires more elaborate devices by bypassing immediately higher authorities. The question also arises whether the procedures by which subordinates control access to the "old man" are sufficiently flexible to permit an informal upward flow of communications. The tendency in all organizations is to protect the chief executive from being unduly bothered; in the military, because formal rank and hierarchy is so clear-cut, informal access to higher-ups can be greatly reduced.

But again it is the possibility of combat, and not hierarchical organization, that produces the command and communications patterns found in the military. The business of the military is grave and deadly serious. Military control develops in an atmosphere where all directives tend to be expressed as authoritative and obligatory. Yet as the nature of modern warfare has become revolutionized, the traditional concepts of organizational control become outmoded. Just as the tactical commander must react to the dilemmas of his role and abandon traditional discipline, so higher echelons must develop new concepts of command. In order to coordinate complex operations, military command becomes tempered with military management—a concept that implies greater reliance on persuasion and negotiation. The tendency to resist these organizational changes in the military establishment is concentrated among officers in the middle ranks. At the bottom of the hierarchy, the realities of combat or training force leaders to adapt; at the very top, the pressures come from the outside and leaders are selected because of their inclination to innovate. But in the middle range, divorced from these pressures and often aware that their prospects of selection to the top are declining, leaders are most likely to develop a defensive stance. Instead of constructive problem-solving, their concern with maintaining the formal prerogatives of rank leads to organizational rigidity, ceremonialism, and retreat from administrative responsibility.

Organizational rigidity in the military establishment is most clearly manifested by the continued efforts of elements of the higher command to reinstitute traditional forms of organizational control when these forms are no longer effective. The

requirements of the cold war have prevented the military establishment from drifting away from a concern about the forms of
discipline necessary for combat relations. The lessons about the
need for tactical initiative are best kept alive in those units whose
routine training most closely approximates actual combat or is
hazardous. Nevertheless, the pressure to reestablish the discipline
of the "old days" is continually present. Often leaders who see
their particular weapons becoming obsolete, and who see no
approach to regaining their organizational dominance, are the
most ritualistic and compulsive about the older forms of military
command; for example, the cavalry colonel in the interwar years,
and more recently, even among aircraft carrier commanders.

The Womble Committee of the Department of Defense which
sought to investigate the professional status of officers as an after-
math of the Korean conflict issued a report in 1953 that contained
strong overtones of concern to revive traditional forms of organizational discipline and officer prerogatives.[2] The report, written
as a reaction to the reforms of the Doolittle Board, not only dealt
with basic matters of pay and promotion but expressed an emphasis on formalism which seemed to be more oriented toward
ideology than to the realities of military life. The need for discipline and command based on domination has been emphasized
in some quarters in the United States military establishment as an
answer to the lack of realistic training and preparation of troops
during the first phases of the Korean conflict. However, in fact,
realistic training that had little or nothing to do with formal
discipline produced in Korea one of the most effective military
forces in recent American history. The performance of military
units in Korea is a striking example of the conditions under which
civilian apathy was prevented from influencing battle behavior
by the performance of a professional officer corps, especially the
junior members, who were convinced that their organizational
integrity was at stake.

A return to organizational control based on domination can
be achieved only at a high cost. In a totalitarian society it can be
achieved because of the repressive political control that is available. Given the cultural traits of American society, the officer

corps runs the risk of losing its most creative intellects while the noncommissioned ranks, as discipline becomes harsher, would attract those who are unsuccessful in civilian life. Any widespread and conscious effort to reimpose stricter discipline is blocked by the political pressures available to selectees.

Since any serious return to rigid organizational controls and discipline based on domination is blocked by the realities of military life and by civilian pressures, nostalgia for the past expresses itself in increased ceremonialism. The opportunities and evidence for increased ceremonialism are ample—from the reintroduction of the dress sword for naval officers to more close order military parades.

Ceremonialism can be functional if it contributes to a sense of self-esteem and to solidarity. From a social psychological point of view ceremonialism is among other things a device for dealing with the fear of death. But at what point does ceremonialism interfere with realistic requirements? Much of the ceremony seems to be a device for avoiding concern with the unsolved problems of military management.

Under pressure to adapt to new requirements, the dilemmas of military command can also lead to a retreat from administrative responsibility. The greater the pressure for organizational change, the more feasible it becomes for officer personnel to claim that new problems are outside their jurisdiction and require directives from higher authorities. Because of the greater speed in communications, decision-making tends to become more centralized. But is there a greater tendency for passing decisions up the line in the military establishment than in other types of organizations? Not a single empirical study exists comparing the military with business or other types of organization on this question, yet such studies would seem to be a first step in assessing the relevance of so-called principles of business administration for military organization.

Role Conflicts

Organizational control in the military establishment extends beyond command channels and internal communications. Every soldier has other roles which can potentially weaken his ability to perform his military obligations. The management of these role conflicts in order to keep them in bounds has become a major effort of military authority. The attraction of an alternative civilian career, the obligations of family, and the cross pressures generated by civilian community contacts are at the root of these role conflicts. Compared with the military profession at the turn of the century, there is every reason to assume that such role conflicts are now more disruptive. A small, homogeneous, isolated professional group is less likely to be subjected to role conflicts. The civilianization of the military, as well as the growth in the size of the military establishment, weakens organizational control over the individual soldier and officer.

As indicated in Chapter II, Hierarchy and Authority, the revolution in military technology has increased the transferability of skills between military and civilian employment. Even for those military personnel who have no specifically transferable skill, the general management skills that life in the military develops are more applicable to civilian employment today than a half-century ago. As a result, military personnel has greater opportunity to shift from its military attachments to civilian enterprise, and organizational control is thereby weakened. There has always been a steady movement of personnel out of the military establishment. Among West Point graduates, comparable statistics on resignations show a gradual increase in recent decades. The professional soldier is also more aware of the possibilities of transfer and is more likely to consider and to reconsider the possibility at various points in his career. Professional officers are continually availing themselves of training at civilian universities and through military educational arrangements to improve their chances for transfer even if they do not actually wish to transfer. The closer links between military institutions and civilian business and universities throw the typical officer into situations where essential contacts can be made.

Family pressures serve to increase role conflicts. Military assignments involve constant rotation from one installation to another, and with each move, disruptions are created, for the role of being a father is not necessarily in tune with being a professional soldier. While shifting of assignments is also a feature of large-scale civilian enterprise, the frequency and distance of military transfers seems to create more family pressures. Powerful role conflicts in family life are generated in units constantly on the alert and under strenuous training assignments. The stresses and strains that role conflicts generate among the crews in the Strategic Air Command were surveyed in a monograph by Ruth Lindquist, *Marriage and Family Life of Officers and Airmen in a Strategic Air Command Wing*.[3] Because of the strains of training and disruption to family life connected with sudden overseas assignments, family tensions become a factor affecting operational readiness, and thereby a concern of Air Force commanders.

In the past, garrison life meant an intermingling of place of residence and place of work, especially during peacetime. The military community had a strong sense of social solidarity and offered extensive mutual assistance to its member families. While garrison life may have isolated the military from civilian influences, it was a device for coping with the role conflicts and tensions that the military family had to face. But, as the military becomes intermingled with civilian, garrison life changes. Even among the Air Force operational units, the shortage of base housing is so great that many families live in the civilian community. The civilian community is not sensitized to the needs of military families and to their special problems. Living in two worlds, the military family tends to compare its lot with that of the civilian neighbor, often resulting in a sense of dissatisfaction, on the part of the military wife.

Married officers are better able to find their place in the civilian community than are enlisted personnel because of the traditions of social visiting that exist between officer personnel. For enlisted families, the task of adjustment is often more difficult, since there is less of a tradition of social contacts among the families of enlisted personnel. Thus, in a study of the role conflict of a first sergeant in the Air Force, almost universal ambiguity existed concerning the social duties of his wife: Should she, or should she not, take the lead in developing social contacts among the enlisted personnel in her husband's squadron? For the unmarried personnel, there may not be a place in the civilian community except in commercial amusements and casual acquaintanceships of the briefest duration.[4]

These role conflicts, especially the conflict between military occupation and the attraction of civilian opportunities, are a primary factor in the turnover of military personnel. As would be expected, the turnover is greatest where the skill is more nearly equivalent to that in civilian employment—noncommissioned officers with electronic specialties. In fact, according to a detailed personnel survey completed for the armed forces by McKinsey and Company, in September, 1956, the average rate of turnover of personnel in the military establishment is no higher than for industry, except in this one category. Turnover, resulting from role conflicts, is simply more disruptive to an organization which requires such high levels of social cohesion.

To reduce these strains, the military establishment must render on an organized basis many of the social services rendered informally in the traditional military garrison. Indeed striking is the extent to which the military establishment has many of the features of the welfare state, without which these role conflicts would become most disruptive. While private commercial interests are continually criticizing the military for its post exchanges and for its welfare services, these features are important sources of institutional control. The American Medical Association looks askance at the family services that military doctors perform. However, regardless of financial considerations, the military doctor must perform the functions of the civilian family doctor, since the military family has fragile roots in the civilian community. In the Air Force, the Dependent Aid Program brings into play a team of specialists whose job is to prevent family disruption in a way suggestive of professional social work practice.

The chaplain and the psychiatrist, with their loose relationship to the channels of command, have the task of reducing by indirect and "therapeutic techniques" the role conflicts of military life. The impact of the psychiatrist on military life is indeed considerable. He becomes an important arbiter as to what constitutes appropriate behavior and how defiant behavior will be treated. Delinquency, anti-social behavior, and nonconformity are not regarded merely as problems in military law but as psychiatric issues. The strength of the psychiatrists depends on their high prestige as medical men and their privileged positions as members of a profession which is located outside the military. These advantages make it possible for them to circumvent and modify military authority. From a suggestive study of the "Role Conflicts of Military Chaplains," by Waldo Burchard, the inference can be drawn that the chaplain in his role as "social worker" is not so effective as the psychiatrist.[5] Often he overidentifies or completely accepts the official military perspective and has less of a sphere of independent influence.

Indoctrination

An indirect source of organizational control is the ideological indoctrination to which the military exposes its personnel. Ideological indoctrination in the military has three quite different elements—(1) the professional code of military behavior, (2) the strategic concepts of military operations, including a description of the enemy, and (3) the political objectives of U.S. national security policy. While the professional code of the military officer is subjected to great strain from within and without the military establishment, a sense of honor goes a long way in explaining organizational control in the armed forces. However, since it is traditional to assume that the armed forces should be nonpolitical in a democracy, efforts to develop an ideological concept of the military mission have met with little success and have perhaps been a source of confusion.

The military forces of the United States had their origins in a revolutionary political movement—in an anti-colonial struggle— yet their professional code of behavior derives from the aristocratic forms against which they struggled. Dedicated patriotism, an almost mystical allegiance to national identity, political conservatism, and a sense of personal fealty to the chief sovereign— the president instead of king—have been among the basic elements of this code. The professional code of the military is now compatible with technical training and expertise, but, basically, the military code prepares the soldier for a "heroic career" and not merely for a specific technical occupation.

If the professional code of the military arose out of aristocratic traditions of fealty, it has had to modify its symbolic content. The professional code of the military is, so to speak, a self-generating one seeking to draw inspiration from its own historical achievements, its religious devotion, and its sense of fraternity. For these purposes, military history is not reality; it is not the account of personal rivalries among competing generals, nor the account of the failures of the War of 1812 or the Spanish-American War, although the armed forces study these errors. It is an interpretation of past events designed to prove that the military profession is an honorable profession. The role of religion in fashioning the American military profession is complex and almost wholly uncharted by social historians. From religious sources, it has found justification for its sense of missionary zeal, its concern with authority and, of course, solace for its suffering.

But it is the sense of fraternity in the military professional code that strikes the sociologist. A sense of intimacy and social solidarity among the officer corps is basic to the professional code. While other professional groups speak of a sense of community, none rivals the military in this respect. Much of military education seems to be concerned with this sense of group solidarity. But clearly after World War II, the military profession experienced a crisis in its sense of professional fraternity. The increase in size and the greater heterogeneity of social background and careers weakened the sense of fraternity. In the Air Force this weakening has been the most pronounced and most troublesome, and has led to the most concern with the sources of an appropriate ethic.[6]

Since the indoctrination of the professional code is slow and continuous, and since it applies to every aspect of military life, conscious efforts to improve professional indoctrination have a high chance of success. But the contemporary efforts of the military to implant in the professional and the citizen soldier a conception of a political goal beyond that of defense of country—

that is, the effort to explain why we fight—have been more irrelevant than unsuccessful.

Strategic issues and ideological images are elements of combat effectiveness and organizational control. The findings of sociologists on the crucial importance of primary group cohesion in military morale do not overlook or eliminate the role of secondary identifications, although some of the enthusiasts of small group research seem to arrive at such a conclusion. Conceptions of the enemy, the strength of nationalism, and the definition of war aims have varying effects depending on military realities. For the bulk of the troops, these factors are secondary to the immediate social organization of military life. These secondary symbols are at best filtered through networks of primary group contact on which individual soldiers depend. If the image of the enemy and the goals of war can be interpreted in terms that are relevant and meet the day-to-day needs of the individual soldier, then ideological indoctrination may succeed. When the Nazi propaganda officers spoke of the advantages of National Socialism as an ideology, their words fell on deaf ears, but when they spoke of how Hitler had abolished unemployment, they were able to reenforce old loyalties among those who had suffered economic distress.

Moreover, in military society as well as in civilian society, there is a very small "hard core" of politically oriented persons. These opinion leaders are often more concerned with the strategic outlines of warfare and are more politically alert. In the totalitarian armies they are the personnel who received years and years of indoctrination in political schools and in party work. Their equivalents are not regarded as essential for democratic armies, nor can they be expected to develop by a few superficial lectures.

Present evidence offers no basis for assuming that political indoctrination of American troops will make them better fighters or more resistant to Communist indoctrination after capture. By political indoctrination we mean implanting a comprehensive dogma which supplies answers to a wide variety of issues. Such indoctrination of the rank and file of the armed forces of a democratic country may have the opposite effect. As Albert Biderman concludes from his study of Air Force prisoners captured in Korea, resistance to Communist doctrine was lodged in the traditional American negativism toward dogma.[7] Any effort at political indoctrination in order to increase organizational control, or to prepare personnel for resisting Communist indoctrination in the event of capture, may have negative consequences if it undermines the American general distrust of dogmas and makes the men feel inferior because they are uninformed, or feel guilty because they are apolitical, vis-à-vis skilled propagandists.

NOTES TO CHAPTER V

[1] One interesting and highly systematic effort to investigate this problem is James D. Thompson's "Authority and Power in 'Identical' Organizations," *American Journal of Sociology*, vol. 62, November, 1956, pp. 290–301. Dealing with Air Force squadrons, Thompson demonstrates that differences between the units are due to differences in perceptions of technical operations and not because of personal relations. This study falls into the category of those that fail to take into consideration the special characteristics of military units—the effects of combat goal.

[2] Department of Defense, *Final Report*—Ad Hoc Committee on the Future of Military Service as a Career That Will Attract and Retain Capable Career Personnel. Press Release, December 3, 1953.

[3] Lindquist, Ruth, *Marriage and Family Life of Officers and Airmen in a Strategic Air Command Wing*. Technical Report no. 5, Air Force Base Project, Institute for Research in Social Science, University of North Carolina, Chapel Hill, October, 1952.

[4] Hunter, Floyd, *Host Community and Air Force Base*. Air Force Base Project, Institute for Research in Social Science, University of North Carolina, Chapel Hill, November, 1952.

[5] Burchard, Waldo W., "Role Conflicts of Military Chaplains," *American Sociological Review*, vol. 19, October, 1954, pp. 528–535.

[6] Wolverton, Wallace I., Lt. Col. (Chaplain), *Ethical Judgments of a Group of Air Force Officers*, Air University, Maxwell Air Force Base, Ala., 1950; also *Behavior Standards in USAFE Personnel*, Report no. HR-18, Human Resources Research Institute, Maxwell Air Force Base, Ala., August, 1952.

[7] Biderman, Albert D., *Effects of Communist Indoctrination Attempts:* Some Comments Based on an Air Force Prisoners of War Study. Document no. 134247, Air Force Personnel and Training Research Center, Lackland Air Force Base, Texas, September, 1947, p. v.

VI

THE SOLDIER AND
INTERNATIONAL RELATIONS

Any extensive effort by the military at political indoctrination of its rank and file beyond clarifying strategic concepts is not appropriate for a political democracy. Nor are such efforts certain to improve military effectiveness. Yet it is clear that the professional officer requires considerable sensitivity to the political and social consequences of military operations. At each step in the graduated application of force, threatened or actual, to the control of international relations, political and social factors are completely intertwined with what has been called military considerations. In varying degrees this has always been the case. But today military administration permits a very small margin of political and social miscalculation. Assuming a perfect and complete form of civilian supremacy, the implementation of military policy is so complex that important political and social tasks tend to adhere to the military even in peacetime. The conduct of troops stationed abroad, the management of foreign assistance programs, and the implementation of military alliances are as much political and social arrangements as they are military operations.

Military leaders in the United States over recent decades have been developing a concern for the political and social implications of their behavior. But to be concerned with these problems does not imply that they have the tradition, the knowledge, or the resources at their disposal, to act on the basis of their concerns. To even the most superficial observer of the military establishment, it is clear that the American military elite does not correspond to the stereotype of a power elite bent on a secret conspiracy. The military elite over the past decades, like the civilian elite groups, has had to broaden its horizon to include the entire spectrum of international relations. It is incorrect to assume that all forms of militarism involve "designed militarism." Designed militarism—the type identified with Prussian militarism—involves the modification and destruction of civilian institutions by military leaders acting directly and premeditatedly through the state and other institutions. Equally significant and more likely to account for crucial aspects of contemporary American problems, is "unanticipated militarism." Unanticipated militarism develops from a lack of effective traditions and practices for controlling the military establishment, as well as from a failure of civilian political leaders to act relevantly and consistently. Under such circumstances a vacuum is created, which not only encourages an extension of the tasks and power of military leadership but actually forces such trends.

But there is every reason, for better or for worse, that the concern with political and social aspects of military operations—in particular, with the limitation on force—is likely to continue, although it is still a question as to how realistic such a concern will be. One can say for better, since it could contribute to a rational foreign policy; for worse, because politically sensitive military leadership could be more difficult to subject to civilian control.

New Professional Perspectives

Basically, the new concerns of the professional soldier arise out of the changed character of international relations, and the new limitations on force. Immediately after the explosion of the atomic bomb, the military concept of international relations was dominated by the potentiality of total war. But as these potentials in international relations were developed, mutual deterrence had the consequence of inhibiting total war. Limited nuclear warfare suddenly emerged as a concept for influencing and controlling international relations. Limited nuclear warfare is a possibility, although the dangers of its developing into general nuclear warfare are so great that it serves mainly as a transitional concept back to limited nonnuclear warfare. In the modern age even nonnuclear warfare differs from such warfare in the prenuclear age, in that all decisions about nonnuclear limited war must now be made with a view to the possibility that such war may develop into a nuclear war—limited or all-out. Limited traditional warfare has, in fact, been the kind of warfare that has occurred during the period of the development of atomic weapons. (Limited warfare would include all forms of armed intervention, irregular warfare, armed subversion, and the control of armed subversion by various means including counter subversion.) Coupled with the reemergence of a concern with the concept of limited warfare— nuclear and nonnuclear—some military thinking is taking place on the strategy and tactics of mutual warning, inspection, and disarmament systems. Both inspection-disarmament and limited warfare as types of military operations are demonstrations in which political and social considerations predominate.

At the same time, the changes that have been described in the internal social organization of the military establishment also force the professional soldier to be more attuned to the political and social aspects of military operations. As has been pointed out: (1) *There has been a shift in the basis of organizational authority, from discipline based on domination to organizational control involving manipulation. New techniques of leadership involve managerial skills, and the ability to develop positive organizational loyalties. Successful military authority requires effective participation at all levels in the hierarchy.* (2) *There has been a narrowing of the skill differential between military and civilian occupations.* In addition, a third factor can be pointed out; namely, *there has been a broadening of the base of officer recruitment.* Military leadership has been shifting its recruitment from a narrow, relatively high-status base to a broader, lower-status, and more representative social base.[1]

The consequences of these trends imply that the professional soldier is required more and more to acquire skills and orientations common to civilian administrators and even to political leaders. Professionalism as a measure of adaptation to social change thereby implies that the classic distinction and tension between the troop commander—the manager of men and machines and the staff officer—the manager of plans and coordination—tend to become less clear-cut. If the preparation for combat requires authority oriented to maintaining initiative among groups and possessing the skills of indirect control, then the skills of the combat commander and the staff officer are in effect converging. One is struck by the number of high-ranking officers in the United States who have combined achievement in both spheres of the military establishment as a result of their World War II and Korean experiences.

Thus, the professional commander becomes more interested in the interpersonal techniques of organization, maintenance of morale, and negotiation. Not only must the professional soldier develop new skills necessary for internal management; he must also develop a "public relations" aptitude, in order to relate and explain his formation to other military formations. This is not to imply that these skills are found among all top military professionals, but that there has been a growth in the concentration of such military commanders. Among them, the potentialities exist for military leadership more sensitive to the political and social aspects of its operations.

These observations do not hide the fact that an important element of tension still exists between the emotional and technical requirements of many of the initial assignments of a combat officer—such as the fighter pilot, or paratrooper—and the requirements of a higher command. Yet for many of those who survive the rigors of indoctrination, training, and initial assignment, the career of professional officer holds the prospect for developing general managerial skills applicable to a wide range of assignments, including politically oriented ones.

These trends may obscure counter trends which are likely to produce new strains in the military establishment and to block the development of broader perspectives. Emerging tensions within the military establishment may well separate those leaders with broad managerial orientations toward their tasks from those who are concerned with the technical development of new weapons systems. Many competent officers are following a scientific and technical career. Their number is growing, their prestige rising, and their position in the hierarchy assured. These scientific specialists have narrow definitions of their tasks and are relatively unconcerned with the political and social implications of the weapons systems which are developing. Their prestige in scientific matters permits them to pass judgment on other issues for which their experiences have not adequately equipped them. Research into career lines and career development in the military establishment is required in order to understand these trends and their consequences. Such research must be broader than personnel selection research and must focus on organizational change.

It is beyond the scope of this bulletin even to touch on the problems of training and indoctrinating military personnel about the political and social consequences of military operations. It is equally beyond the scope of this bulletin even to touch on the problems of modifying our civilian political controls so as to integrate effectively military leadership with the other officials managing U.S. foreign policy. It is relevant, however, to point to elements of sociological thinking, broadly conceived, which have potentials for providing knowledge about the likely political and social consequences of military operations. Unfortunately, it cannot be said that professional sociologists have devoted sufficient efforts to these matters. The sociological aspect of military institutions and the sociological dimensions of international relations are at best peripheral to the interests of most sociologists. For a graduate student to be interested in, and to pursue, such topics for his doctoral dissertation is all too frequently regarded as a form of deviant behavior.

Consequences of Force

Thus far the focus of this study has been on the internal structure of the military establishment as a social system and as a reflection of the larger civilian society. When one begins to speak of the consequences of military behavior, the political and social outcomes, the frame of reference broadens. The military specialist thinks of force as a factor in international relations in absolute quantitative and physical terms—manpower and firepower. The sociologist must assume that in addition to military force there are a variety of means that a nation state has at its disposal for influencing international relations: economic, cultural and political media, diplomatic negotiation, mass persuasion, to mention a few. Of crucial importance to the sociologist is the particular organization of these various means, for the same instruments differently organized have different consequences.

For example, military occupation by American forces carrying their own logistical support have had very different political consequences from those resulting from occupation by Russian troops who exploit the local resources. American military government, from Germany to Korea, was deeply influenced not only by the political directives under which it operated; the character of its performance was heavily influenced by the fact that military government organization was kept strictly parallel to tactical military organization. Consequently, as the front expanded, specific localities were administered by as many as four different units, each having to rebuild its own local contacts. Even after stabilization, or where military government took over major areas directly as in Japan and Korea, the channels of command were unduly complicated by their articulation with occupational units. The entire setup tended to result in an emphasis on technical efficiency at the expense of social and political objectives.

The utilization of a sociological perspective has been limited chiefly to those functions which the military has considered to be secondary functions—political and psychological warfare, military government, and troop indoctrination. With the exception of economics, the use of the theoretical and technical capabilities of social scientists in dealing with military problems has been sporadic and infrequent at best, although notable instances can be reported by social scientists now out of uniform. This is a further reflection of the compartmentalization of military thinking from political and social concepts. More often than not, the social scientist is accepted and thought to be relevant by military authority because of his substantive knowledge, as a sort of intelligence officer.

The relevance of sociological thinking is not limited to the analysis of consequences of particular military operations. It has a broader relevance for understanding the potentials and limitations on the use of force in all its dimensions as a factor for influencing international relations. Force in international relations involves a cycle of steps: strategical and operational planning, the direction of military operations, the consolidation of military outcome, and the assessment of military effects. At each point in the cycle, political and sociological assumptions are required; and at each point the perspectives of the sociologist are relevant.

In the past, the political and sociological assumptions that military planners have made either remained implicit or were limited to their stereotypes as to how soldiers of specific nationalities behaved in battle. These stereotypes often were based on the contacts that professional soldiers developed in the course of their careers, as military observers, military attachés, and participants in previous military operations. When nations fought with limited military forces, and the issue at stake was the likely effectiveness of military units in being, such estimates at least supplied some basis for military planning. But as warfare grew to require total involvement of the population, the problem extends well beyond the scope of traditional military thinking. The U.S. military services entered World War II unprepared to handle such estimates in their strategical planning. During the course of the hostilities, the evaluation of strategic intelligence was developed to the point that highly sophisticated estimates of the probable behavior of German and Japanese social systems under attack were developed. In retrospect, these estimates had high relevance and validity, although the extent to which they entered into actual strategical planning and operations is most problematical. Many of these estimates were developed by civilian social scientists in uniform and were often the results of self-generated assignments, which ultimately developed some organizational legitimacy.

Since the end of World War II the requirement of strategic political and social intelligence for guiding national security policy, including military policy, has been an accepted assumption. For a period the armed forces even played a role in subsidizing university-based social research on foreign social systems, as for example the Russian research program of the U.S. Air

Force at Harvard University. The theoretical dimensions and the practical requirements of strategic intelligence for foreign policy is a topic that evokes strong and passionate opinions among experts especially in a period of difficult foreign relations, since it is easier to declare that intelligence was faulty than to reevaluate policies.

But the fact of the matter is that sociological analysis of total societies is not yet adequately developed to clarify these basic issues. Current sociological analysis tends to view violence in a social system as a form of disorganization or as deviant behavior.[2] It is also important to note that such an orientation is prevalent among social anthropologists, even though a major source of social change among primitive social systems has been warfare. As a result, a body of propositions about the conditions under which force maintains and modifies social structure has not yet been developed.

Given the present state of sociological theory, one feasible approach to a more systematic understanding of the role of force in social change is the comparative sociological study of military organization; that is, all types of military organization, including paramilitary forces, guerrilla units, and resistance movements. A model for such research can be found in the analysis of the guerrillas in Malaya by Lucian Pye.[3] An alternative frame of reference is to focus on military elites as a social grouping and to analyze their social composition, career lines, and indoctrination as an index to military behavior.[4]

The direction of military operations requires an economy of effort in order to avoid needless slaughter and to maximize the chances of achieving political and social objectives. Force cannot be applied effectively merely in terms of military considerations. With the destructive prospects of atomic warfare, force has meaning only as it relates to efforts at persuasion. The British term "political warfare" is an effort to conceptualize the use of persuasion and propaganda techniques in a military context.

Among Americans there is a belief that the United States has no tradition and skill in international communications in support of its military objectives. The word "propaganda" is thought of as foreign to U.S. customs and repulsive to U.S. objectives. Control and effective management of political warfare are most complex for a democratic state. Wide areas of political warfare require an element of secret preparation, at least, and secrecy is disruptive of democratic political control. However, it is incorrect to assume that the United States is without a tradition in international political warfare. American history from the time of the Revolutionary Era is replete with examples of imaginative and successful exploitation of persuasive means to achieve military objectives. *A Psychological Warfare Casebook* documents these events and at the same time seeks to set forth the extent to which social scientific perspectives are relevant for developing principles for conducting psychological warfare.[5] One of the most important changes in political warfare techniques has been the development of large and complex organizational machinery. Whereas, historically, propaganda could be disseminated by a few key figures and leaders, today large staffs and organizations are required. The extensive planning and organization of Soviet communications is documented by Wilbur Schramm and John W. Riley, Jr., in the case of the Korean and Communist occupation of South Korea.[6]

But as long as the military concept of warfare focused on atomic war, the official stimulus for research was on the social and psychological aspects of disaster rather than on political and psychological warfare. Most available civilian disasters have been carefully investigated and important observations systemized by Martha Wolfenstein.[7] With the reemergence of limited warfare concepts, questions about the social consequences of military operations are put in another light. What situations of the past and the present are likely models to clarify future contingencies? Limited warfare, if it has any reality, eliminates the distinction between military operations and the police type of duty. Such has been the nature of every limited war since the end of World War II involving Communist forces. Even the United Nations forces operating in the Israeli-Arab conflict found that more conventional police organization was required to maintain an unstable equilibrium. Communist political doctrine apparently is able to produce organizational forms which are equipped to handle the wide variety of missions that limited warfare requires. Since politics is supreme, the traditions of professional soldiers are not permitted to obstruct radical innovations.

The analysis of the sociological consequences of limited warfare cannot be understood within the categories used by the American military establishment. The military, in an effort to accommodate itself to political needs, has gradually added to its staff a number of specialized auxiliaries: psychological warfare personnel, military government specialists, guerrilla warfare teams. And now personnel are to be trained for military assistance operations. The effectiveness of these specialists depends on U.S. national policies. Yet the concept that these specialists perform separate technical functions has been a fundamental weakness in their support of military operations. It is hardly likely that research on the successes and failures of these politico-military functions in the recent past will bring about dramatic changes in military thinking, although rethinking of past experiences is essential.[8] An understanding of how American social structure has influenced the development of our military institutions and how military organization adapts to and resists change is at the root of the matter.

In the present state of international relations, the military establishment persists in thinking mainly about the implications of future hostilities, limited or total. But the immediate impact of U.S. worldwide military system is in effect determining, or at least fundamentally conditioning, the outcome of the cold war. The U.S. military establishment and its official doctrines have had important consequences in fashioning Soviet strategy and tactics in the nuclear age.[9] The stationing of troops in allied countries and the creation of new elites and counter elites by military assistance programs are equally important aspects of military operations. The conduct of military staffs in international alliances speeds up or retards the development of regional political and economic arrangements. The actual deployment of our air forces, and the public statements—threats and reassurances—that military leaders are daily forced to make, constitute for better or worse the most potent political warfare.

Some public opinion polling has been conducted on the attitudes of allied populations toward the American troops stationed in their country. The work of staff members of the Social Science Division of The Rand Corporation has been a notable example of a sustained research contribution to these problems. Research studies from this group include Hans Speier's analysis of the reactions of the German military elite to remilitarization and U.S. atomic policy, and the case study by W. Phillips Davison of the classic use of the military establishment in the cold war, *The Berlin Blockade:* A Study in Cold War Politics.[10]

But sociologists and members of related disciplines have not accepted the responsibility for the systematic study of the impact of the military, as a social system in being, on the cold war. Under these circumstances it is understandable that the military has not developed a profound interest in these research matters. Moreover, it would be most undesirable in a democracy if the locus of concern was exclusively or even mainly with the military. If social change, at home and abroad, is a central theme of sociological analysis, the implications are obvious.

NOTES TO CHAPTER VI

[1] Janowitz, Morris, *The Professional Soldier.* In preparation.

[2] Such a perspective is even to be found by implication in the highly systematic works of Talcott Parsons. See *The Social System,* The Free Press, Glencoe, Ill., 1951.

[3] Pye, Lucian W., *Guerilla Communism in Malaya:* Its Social and Political Meaning. Princeton University Press, Princeton, N. J., 1956.

[4] An example to this approach is to be found in Ithiel de Sola Pool's *The Satellite Generals:* A Study of Military Elites in the Soviet Sphere, Stanford University Press, Stanford, Calif., 1955.

[5] Daugherty, William E., and Morris Janowitz, *A Psychological Warfare Casebook.* The Johns Hopkins University Press, Baltimore, 1958.

[6] Schramm, Wilbur, and John W. Riley, Jr., "Communication in the Sovietized State as Demonstrated in Korea," *American Sociological Review,* vol. 16, December, 1951, pp. 757–766.

[7] Wolfenstein, Martha, *Disaster.* The Free Press, Glencoe, Ill., 1957.

[8] Meade, Grant E., *American Military Government in Korea.* Columbia University Press, New York, 1951.

[9] Garthoff, Raymond, *Soviet Strategy in the Nuclear Age.* Frederick A. Praeger, Inc., New York, 1958.

[10] Speier, Hans, *German Rearmament and Atomic War,* Row, Peterson and Co., Evanston, Ill., 1957; Davison, W. Phillips, *The Berlin Blockade:* A Study in Cold War Politics, Princeton University Press, Princeton, N. J., 1958. The Social Science Research Council has established a Committee on National Security Policy, under Professor William Fox, which stimulates and reflects the interest of historians and political scientists in the analysis of the backgrounds of military policy.

SELECTED BIBLIOGRAPHY

SELECTED BIBLIOGRAPHY

ANDRZEJEWSKI, STANISLAW, *Military Organization and Society*. Routledge and Kegan Paul, London, 1954.

BIDERMAN, ALBERT D., *Effects of Communist Indoctrination Attempts:* Some Comments Based on an Air Force Prisoners of War Study. Document no. 134247, Air Force Personnel and Training Research Center, Lackland Air Force Base, Texas, September, 1947.

BROWN, C. S., *The Social Attitudes of American Generals, 1898–1940*. Unpublished doctoral dissertation, University of Wisconsin, Madison, Wis., 1951.

BURCHARD, WALDO W., "Role Conflicts of Military Chaplains," *American Sociological Review*, vol. 19, October, 1954, pp. 528–535.

CHESLER, DAVID J., NIEL J. VAN STEENBERG, AND JOYCE E. BRUECKEL, "Effect on Morale of Infantry Team Replacement and Individual Replacement Systems," *Sociometry*, vol. 18, December, 1955, pp. 587–597.

CHRISTIE, RICHARD, *An Experimental Study of Modification in Factors Influencing Recruits' Adjustment to the Army*. Research Center for Human Relations, New York University, 1953, mimeographed.

DAUGHERTY, WILLIAM E., AND MORRIS JANOWITZ, *A Psychological Warfare Casebook*. The Johns Hopkins University Press, Baltimore, 1958.

DAVIS, ARTHUR K., "Bureaucratic Patterns in the Navy Officer Corps," *Social Forces*, vol. 27, December, 1948, pp. 143–153.

DAVISON, W. PHILLIPS, *The Berlin Blockade:* A Study in Cold War Politics. Princeton University Press, Princeton, N. J., 1958.

DEMETER, KARL, *Das Deutsche Heer und Seine Offiziere*. Verlag von Reimar Hobbing, Berlin, 1935.

FRANKLIN, JOHN HOPE, *The Militant South, 1800–1861*. Belknap Press of Harvard University Press, Cambridge, Mass., 1956.

HENRY, ANDREW F., AND EDGAR F. BORGATTA, "A Comparison of Attitudes of Enlisted and Commissioned Air Force Personnel," *American Sociological Review*, vol. 18, December, 1953, pp. 669–671.

HENRY, ANDREW F., JOHN W. MASLAND, AND LAURENCE I. RADWAY, "Armed Forces Unification and the Pentagon Officer," *Public Administration Review*, vol. 15, Summer, 1955, pp. 173–180.

HOMANS, GEORGE C., "The Small Warship," *American Sociological Review*, vol. 11, June, 1946, pp. 294–300.

HUMAN BEHAVIOR IN MILITARY SOCIETY, Special Issue of *The American Journal of Sociology*, vol. 51, March, 1946, pp. 359–508.

HUNTER, FLOYD, *Host Community and Air Force Base*. Air Force Base Project, Institute for Research in Social Science, University of North Carolina, Chapel Hill, November, 1952.

HUNTINGTON, SAMUEL P., *The Soldier and the State*. Harvard University Press, Cambridge, Mass., 1957.

JANOWITZ, MORRIS, "Military Elites and the Study of War," *Conflict Resolution*, vol. 1, March, 1957, pp. 9–18.

LEIGHTON, ALEXANDER H., *Human Relations in a Changing World*. E. P. Dutton and Co., New York, 1949.

LEWIS, MICHAEL A., *England's Sea-Officers:* The Story of the Naval Profession. Allen and Unwin, Ltd., London, 1939.

LINDQUIST, RUTH, *Marriage and Family Life of Officers and Airmen in a Strategic Air Command Wing*. Technical Report no. 5, Air Force Base Project, Institute for Research in Social Science, University of North Carolina, Chapel Hill, October, 1952.

LITTLE, ROGER WILLIAM, *A Study of the Relationship Between Collective Solidarity and Combat Role Performance*. Unpublished doctoral dissertation, Michigan State University, East Lansing, Mich., 1955.

MACK, RAYMOND W., *Social Stratification on U.S. Air Force Bases*. Technical Report no. 4, Air Force Base Project, Institute for Research in Social Science, University of North Carolina, Chapel Hill, undated.

MANDELBAUM, DAVID G., "Psychiatry in Military Society," *Human Organization*, vol. 13, Fall, 1954, pp. 5–15; Winter, 1955, pp. 19–25.

MARSHALL, S. L. A., *Men Against Fire*. William Morrow and Co., New York, 1947.

MASLAND, JOHN W., AND LAURENCE I. RADWAY, *Soldiers and Scholars.* Princeton University Press, Princeton, N. J., 1957.

MATTICK, HANS W., *Parole to the Army:* A Research Report on Felons Paroled to the Army During World War II. Presented at the 87th Annual Congress of Corrections in Chicago, Ill., August, 1957.

MEADE, GRANT E., *American Military Government in Korea.* Columbia University Press, New York, 1951.

MERTON, ROBERT K., AND PAUL F. LAZARSFELD, editors, *Studies in the Scope and Method of "The American Soldier."* The Free Press, Glencoe, Ill., 1950.

PAGE, CHARLES H., "Bureaucracy's Other Face," *Social Forces,* vol. 25, October, 1946, pp. 88–94.

POOL, ITHIEL DE SOLA, and others, *The Satellite Generals:* A Study of Military Elites in the Soviet Sphere. Stanford University Press, Stanford, Calif., 1955.

PYE, LUCIAN W., *Guerilla Communism in Malaya:* Its Social and Political Meaning. Princeton University Press, Princeton, N. J., 1956.

REPORT OF THE WORKING GROUP ON HUMAN BEHAVIOR UNDER CONDITIONS OF MILITARY SERVICE: A Joint Project of the Research and Development Board and the Personnel Policy Board in the Office of the Secretary of Defense. Washington, June, 1951.

SCHRAMM, WILBUR, AND JOHN W. RILEY, JR., "Communication in the Sovietized State as Demonstrated in Korea," *American Sociological Review,* vol. 16, December, 1951, pp. 757–766.

SEGAL, J., *Factors Related to the Collaboration and Resistance Behavior of U.S. Army PW's in Korea.* Technical Report no. 33, Human Resources Research Office, George Washington University, Washington, D. C., December, 1956.

SELVIN, HANAN CHARLES, *The Effects of Leadership Climate on the Non-Duty Behavior of Army Trainees.* Unpublished doctoral dissertation, Columbia University, New York, 1956.

SHARTLE, C. L., "Studies in Naval Leadership: Part I" in *Groups, Leadership and Men,* edited by Harold S. Guetzkow. Carnegie Press, Pittsburgh, 1951, pp. 119–133.

SHILS, EDWARD S., AND MORRIS JANOWITZ, "Cohesion and Disintegration in the Wehrmacht in World War II," *Public Opinion Quarterly,* vol. 12, Summer, 1948, pp. 280–315.

SPEIER, HANS, *German Rearmament and Atomic War*. Row, Peterson and Co., Evanston, Ill., 1957.

SPEIER, HANS, *Social Order and the Risks of War*. George W. Stewart, New York, 1952.

STOUFFER, SAMUEL A., and others, *The American Soldier*. Princeton University Press, Princeton, N. J., 1949, vols. 1 and 2.

SUCHMAN, EDWARD A., ROBIN M. WILLIAMS, JR., AND ROSE K. GOLD-SEN, "Student Reaction to Impending Military Service," *American Sociological Review*, vol. 18, June, 1953, pp. 293–304.

THOMPSON, JAMES D., "Authority and Power in 'Identical' Organizations," *American Journal of Sociology*, vol. 62, November, 1956, pp. 290–301.

TURNER, RALPH H., "The Naval Disbursing Officer as a Bureaucrat," *American Sociological Review*, vol. 12, June, 1947, pp. 342–348.

VAGTS, ALFRED, *A History of Militarism*. W. W. Norton and Co., New York, 1937.

WILLIAMS, RICHARD HAYS, *Human Factors in Military Operations:* Some Applications of the Social Sciences to Operations Research. Technical Memorandum ORO-T-259, Operations Research Office, Chevy Chase, Md., 1954, mimeographed.

WOLVERTON, WALLACE I., Lt. Col. (Chaplain), *Ethical Judgments of a Group of Air Force Officers*. Air University, Maxwell Air Force Base, Ala., 1950.